You Are The Plan

God's account of your remarkable story

R. J. STAUB

ISBN: 0692843914
ISBN 13: 9780692843918

DEDICATION

To all those saints who may feel they have to do something, become something, or belong to something other than belonging to Jesus Christ, for their life to be significant.

CONTENTS

Acknowledgements   vii
Introduction   ix

1   Beginning at the House   1
2   Retiring a Myth   7
3   The Christian Landscape   11
4   The Church and the Kingdom   30
5   Last Minute Instructions   41
6   'Our Daily Bread'   51
7   Church – a Living Thing   56
8   A Critical Adjustment   63
9   Valuing the Environment   68
10 A Brief Window Into 'The Ministry'   82
11 Keeping it Real   89
12 You are the Plan   98
13 Stepping Up   127
14 A Sampling of Scripture   134
15 A Final Example   138

ACKNOWLEDGEMENTS

It has been suggested that most of what we write we owe to someone else, but we've just forgotten where we read or heard it. I
heartily confess that likelihood. I especially thank Jeanie Staub
for our five wonderful decades together, and how profoundly her
heart for God and His people has shaped my life and perspectives.

My sincere thanks also to Craig Pardue for his insightful cri-
tique, suggestions, and encouragement, and to Michael Staub who
has challenged and refined my ideas, and helped me with the entirety of this project. Significant statements in this text he first
articulated, either in part or whole.

INTRODUCTION

I'm finding myself more and more uncomfortable being associated with the term 'Christianity.' In American culture its connotations have become increasingly parochial, prejudicial, and political. I've been a believer almost all my lifetime, so I want to speak frankly about the message of Jesus Christ, and about what I believe is a widespread distortion and frequent exploitation of His gospel.

Grateful for the privilege of serving the Lord, I have always felt a constraint to diligently and truthfully, at least to the limits my understanding, represent *His* interests in every person and enterprise. What follows is the result of a lifetime of prayerful observation and experience.

There is almost nothing in the words of Jesus Christ to suggest the sprawling religious industry called Christianity in America, or the myriad of forms and practice under the same banner visible throughout the world. Furthermore, it is impossible to extrapolate from His messages to the throngs on the hills of Judea that His vision for them was to create another religious complex that would somehow rival, and eventually outperform Judaism and the competing pagan religions.

Jesus spoke directly, forcefully, to ordinary folks like you and me, challenging them to embrace an entirely new view of reality; a reality which He called 'the Kingdom of God.' Teaching after teaching, parable after parable, He fashioned a conviction in His hearers that they could know God personally and interact with Him in the daily commerce of life.

Delivered with a child's simplicity in a prophetic tone, His 'gospel of the kingdom' was directed toward everyman, from the most humble to the rich and powerful. It crossed every boundary of race, culture, and class, calling men and women to abandon every other allegiance and follow Him. He asked them to believe explicitly what He was teaching, and He assured them if they acted on those things it would result in peace, provision, hope, and something extraordinary which He called 'eternal life.'

Jesus Christ empowered people with His words, His example, and ultimately His Spirit. They became flesh and blood ambassadors of this new kingdom; a kingdom built not by might, money, masses, or manipulation, but by love, humility, and service, one person at a time.

The massive structures of American Christianity convey only a faint suggestion of the majestic life that was Jesus Christ. Almost everything their imposing presence implies was patently rejected by Jesus. He made no effort to configure the crowds into a homogeneous whole for some religious purpose; He taught them, fed them, and sent them home. He never tried to 'own' them in some denominational sense; their loyalty was born of their freedom, and the more they embraced His message the freer they became. The constraints and obligations inherent in His gospel were welcomed in the fresh air of loving acceptance and individual affirmation, so absent in contemporary Judaism. (Matt. 11:29, 30)

Jesus of Nazareth, by Himself, stands higher than any man's vision can take in. His redemptive acts in both life and death completely overshadow Christianity's attempts to embellish their significance with religious decoration, however well intended. His words resound to the core of us, and require a lifetime of devotion to explore their depth.

Much of what American Christianity has constructed, both in word and visible presence, must often be moved aside in order to get a clear and unobstructed look at Jesus Christ. *"Behold! The*

Lamb of God who takes away the sin of the world!" John cried. (John 1:29) Is there any conceivable thing, however rare or holy, that should be allowed to obscure the solitary hope and remedy for our condition? Both the saints and sinners have a right to what institutional religion quite often fails to deliver; clearly expressed in the words of the Greeks to Philip, *"Sir, we wish to see Jesus!"* (John 12:21)

We hope to get a clearer view of Him as we proceed, and we're confident of that since the first thing Jesus said about the kingdom of God is that it has *'come near.'* (Matt. 4:17) That very potent truth, and all it suggests, is the platform for everything in this book.

Is it possible to see the church through a different lens? Is that something we're willing to consider? What if we could envision it more like Jesus seemed to describe it; a loosely structured, grassroots movement; a person/family centered redemptive organism which functions and grows quite naturally under the direction of God's Spirit? What if *true* Christianity only becomes visible as redeemed human beings touch others? We'll see.

In any discussion of contemporary Christianity, it is important to highlight the profound difference between what the term 'church' means in the scriptures, and what it generally means to the American culture and consciousness. The Greek word *Ekklesia*, most often used in the New Testament and translated into English as 'church,' is comprised of two parts: *Ek*, meaning 'out of' and *Klesis*, meaning 'ones who are called.' Therefore, the literal meaning of the biblical term 'church' is *'the ones who are called out.'*

Obviously then, 'church' in the scriptures refers to *people*, or a collection of people. It is never referring to a religious system, a building, a denomination, or an institution of some kind. As far as we can ascertain, these things began to gradually find their way into Christianity a couple of generations after the New Testament was written. So, when the apostles Paul, Peter, James, and John refer to *the church* in their letters, they're talking about the believers, the saints, and not about a 'religious' anything. They saw the purpose and work of God as a divine movement in and among *the people*, and that is precisely how I understand and generally use the term.

We must, however, communicate about the world as we find it, and in 21ˢᵗ century America that brings us face to face with this highly developed ecclesiastical system and infrastructure called "Christianity." This great diversity of Christian organizations and structures is *not* the church, but has been created to help the church facilitate her mission to serve Jesus Christ. How effectively and faithfully these Christian institutions *actually do that* is a significant part of this inquiry.

At the outset I want to discourage any notion that this is a treatise opposing organized Christianity; that some sort of *dis*-organized expression of the church were somehow more appealing or spiritual. However, just as Paul challenged the Corinthian believers to 'examine' themselves at the Lord's Table so their participation was 'worthy' (1 Cor. 11:27, 28), self-examination regarding our corporate approach and service to God is surely warranted on a consistent basis as well.

I genuinely appreciate the kingdom potential of organized churches, ministries, and mission organizations, and *it is not the intent of this book, either by statement or implication, to move believers away from organized Christianity.* Who would want to do harm to his family simply because they were having differences, or were dysfunctional in some ways? Both Jeanie and I were raised in relatively traditional Christian settings, and our debt to the many saints who influenced our lives during those days is immeasurable. We value the positive efforts of the organized churches.

Rather, the content of this work is directed toward individual believers (and anyone seeking to better understand the message of Jesus), offering an honest and informed perspective about the church as we're generally experiencing it in our culture, and a strenuous encouragement for them to re-evaluate its mission, priorities, and effectiveness in light of the New Testament teachings and examples. Every reader is urged to prayerfully consider this material and to respond appropriately.

In my view, what is at issue in this discussion is, first of all, the future *viability* of the organized church, and second, and more important, the declaration and preservation of freedom and kingdom function for the saints. There's no silver bullet, no magic, no 'deeper revelation' in these pages; just some simple, straightforward encouragement to forge a relationship with Jesus Christ; one tempered in your own furnace, and shaped with your own hammer. By saying that I'm suggesting there are clear choices open to the saints that allow them to engage God daily in a non-prescriptive way which will ultimately lead them into a free, distinctly unique, and truly abundant life. (John 10:10)

Again, I'm not hoping to 'repackage' the faith, but I definitely want to persuade you to honestly *rethink it*. Here is what I can say conclusively from Jesus' words and the supporting New Testament scriptures: God is ultimately working His will in the earth, the risen Jesus Christ is Lord over it all, the Holy Spirit is here to help you, and **You Are the Plan.**

Your story is important, substantial. There is a depth to you, a dimension of spirit you can't see or understand that God purposes to awaken through your contact with Jesus Christ. The movements of God's Spirit in your life are as kingdom strategic as that of any believer. Whether you're a priest or a postman, a Senator or a seamstress, God has set in motion through your faith in Christ a holy process through which you may gain enlightenment, enrichment, and kingdom significance. Your journey with Jesus is a

God-conceived documentary that chronicles His redeeming grace before a watching world.

Your earnest responses to the Word and the Spirit will detail, with kingdom precision, the unfolding plan of God. Even your mishaps and blunders will color the narrative with testimony to God's mercy and providence. Corrie Ten Boom, who lost her family as she suffered through the horrors of Nazi camps to become a world-wide ambassador for Christ put it simply; *"God's plans are perfect!"*

The account of your journey may never be published, but you may be sure significant parts of it are being observed and examined, both in heaven and on earth (Eph. 3:9-11; 1 Peter 1:12). What happens with you *matters!* Indeed, your body and mind, your character, personality, motivations, understanding, and spiritual insights are the living foundation God will use to fulfill His purposes. And in rhythm with your own experience will be the influence you exert on the myriad of other people in your life, all of whom, whether saints or sinners, are also loved and valued by their Creator. *That's the plan of God.*

What follows will outline how this rather simple idea will work in individual lives, and how it may impact a believers' interaction with the church as we know it. As we survey the American church, we'll address these questions:

- What is the 'kingdom of God,' and is it synonymous with what we call 'church?'
- Who has God appointed to represent Him and His gospel in the world?
- Who is responsible for the administration of God's kingdom?
- How significant am I, as an individual believer, in God's redemptive activity?

- What is my relationship to organized Christianity?
- What is a Christian's primary source of leadership and guidance?
- As a faith community, are we building what the scriptures command us to build?
- Are pastors, evangelists, teachers, and prophets found only in the institutional church?
- How can problems in the church be impacted in a positive and peaceful way?
- Will understanding these things benefit my life significantly?

These are just a few of the issues we will focus on, concluding with a challenge for believers to become pioneers in *"a Christianity that is neither polished nor pre-packaged, but will have the scars and bruises, the duty-worn tools, and the firm grip of blue collar saints . . . ."* We've purposed, by God's grace, to recover for the believers, and hopefully for our churches, the revolutionary message and assignment Jesus entrusted to us.

"Immanuel," *God with us*, was the most stunning event in human history. Yet it occurred in an obscure place, among a subjugated people, with little fanfare or spectacle. A few foreign astrologers, and some bewildered shepherds were the only ones getting anything to gawk at. The humble parentage and upbringing of Jesus of Nazareth demonstrates how often God acts through quiet process rather than dramatic events. I attach great significance to that fact in laying out the proposition; **You are the Plan.**

For Christian readers, this as an appeal; a brother's invitation to consider again the mission of Jesus of Nazareth and our participation in it. Hopefully these thoughts will help refine and solidify your own understanding and appreciation of His gospel.

And if you're a non-believer, or perhaps you're wondering exactly where Jesus fits into all the conflicting claims and forms of American Christianity, I hope you'll gain some perspective that will aid you in your enquiry into the meaning of His remarkable life.

For the sake of brevity, and (I hope) clarity, I will avoid religious terminology and theology, relying on the scriptures to speak for themselves. So, I offer what follows, instructed and moderated by these cautions from the Apostle and the Lord:

> **1 Corinthians 3:9-13** – Paul taught there is a single foundation upon which to build one's life and that is a relationship with Jesus Christ. That foundation he carefully laid into the hearts of the believers. *"But,* he cautions, *"Let each one take heed how he builds on it."* (vs. 10) It is possible, he warns, to build on the message of Jesus a body of work that will not stand the test of Divine evaluation (wood, hay, and straw); *"each one's work will be manifest, for the Day will declare it, because it will be revealed by fire, and the fire will test each one's work, of what sort it is. If anyone's work which he has built on it endures, he will receive a reward. If anyone's work is burned, he will suffer loss, but he himself will be saved . . ."* (vss. 13-15)
>
> **Matthew 13:24-30** – Jesus' parable of the wheat and the tares suggests that as we look at American Christianity we avoid the compulsion to somehow 'fix it!' Embedded in that vast religious complex are many of the precious saints of God; loving, earnest, committed to living out the good things the Lord has deposited in their lives.

Leading them are a host of ministries who, for the most part, want those good folk to prosper in life and in their relation to Christ. So, as we give a critical look at some Christian doctrine and practice, we must carefully guard against doing damage to God's saints and servants. We're challenging *ideas, systems, and traditions,* not people or their motives.

"No," says the parable, *"lest while you gather up the tares you also uproot the wheat with them. Let both grow together until the harvest, and at the time of harvest I will say to the reapers, 'First gather together the tares and bind them in bundles to burn them, but gather the wheat into my barn.'"*

Whether we're grappling with issues inside the church or outside it, our conflict is not with 'flesh and blood.' (Eph. 6:12)

1

BEGINNING AT THE HOUSE

"Now remember, family go light!" My mom would peer over her right shoulder at me in the back seat, making sure I understood the program. She always drove when our family went somewhere; in this case, to church.

Bob and Lois Staub were just a regular Christian couple; friendly, honest, hardworking, and devout. In the 1940's, when they owned Red Rock Poultry farm in Pennsylvania, they often hosted and fed their entire church family. Later, during their years in Phoenix, Bob was a carpenter and Lois a secretary, but they were always about doing good and touching lives. One of my most potent memories of them involves sights, sounds, and smells you never forget; on any given Sunday, watching my Mom making gravy as we prepared to feed and fellowship with a family we'd just met at church.

'Family go light' meant the roast Mom had put in the oven before we left wasn't quite equal to the number of mouths it needed to feed. Since Dad and I were known to consume an entire roast ourselves, a

word of restraint was appropriate as we led our guests to the house for dinner; something they did more Sunday's than not in those days.

Holidays were much the same; a bunch of friends, mixed with strangers or the struggling, joining us for food and fellowship. Most folks were really appreciative, and back then conversation was still preferred over entertainment. There was always lots of laughter.

Dad would thank God for the food and for the souls gathered at his table. His prayer wasn't fancy or long, nor varied much, but it never *sounded* routine; there was always something deeply earnest about it. Conversation usually moved from getting acquainted, and what brought these people to our church, to more personal and spiritual matters. Somehow Bob and Lois made that easier for folks. *Hearts came open around their table.* It reminds me of Paul's commendation of Philemon; *"The hearts of the saints have been refreshed by you, brother!"* (Philemon 7)

The afternoon usually ended with prayer. More than one young ministry couple was encouraged and fortified by a few hours with Bob and Lois, and they frequently left with a bit of money pressed into their hand. Many saints were prayed for, some were healed, or they experienced an encounter with the Spirit of the Lord. I was mostly out of sight during these times, *but I was listening.*

Folks seldom left our house empty handed. I wasn't always sure what our guests took away from the church service that morning, but I sure knew what they'd received when they left Bob and Lois! There was always the love, openness, and warmth that everyone craves, and my Dad and Mom gave these freely and equally to saints and sinners. Our guests also took with them leftovers, fresh flowers, or fruit from our citrus trees . . . and *always* a 'kingdom connection;' a link to a couple of seasoned saints who would try to help them get where they were going.

Raised in the Brethren traditions, Dad's gospel was rooted in holiness, simplicity, and straight-forward commerce with everyone. Mom was a Vermont Methodist who had a profound encounter with the Lord in her twenties and so became, everywhere and always, a strong advocate for the Word and the Spirit. Dad was the rock-solid altar and Mom was the fire, and together they impacted hundreds of lives without ever giving a thought to being 'a ministry.' Married for 50 years, they were the real deal; genuine Jesus people.

Early on I realized my understanding of the gospel took shape by seeing much of the Sermon on the Mount demonstrated in my home growing up. (Matt. 5-7) Often the Apostles insisted that leaders be 'given to hospitality' as part of their qualifications. (Rom. 12:13; 1 Tim. 3:2; Titus 1:8) Peter exhorted *all* the saints, as they sensed challenging times ahead, to 'have company!' (1 Peter 4:7-10, my translation) Whatever gift you have, Peter urged, use it to bless and encourage your brethren. Bob and Lois did that.

I suggest what took place in their lives and home (much like countless other saints around the world) was not a mere prelude to some larger, and more profound spiritual agenda but was instead the 'main event!' Significant in a way reminiscent of Jesus' humble nativity, such simple life transactions are, in God's great providence, quite often transforming and life-defining for the people impacted by them. They are the real 'stuff' of kingdom participation.

Again, as we reflect on the movements and message of Jesus chronicled in the gospels, we are amazed by the confidence He expressed toward ordinary people. *"You are the light of the world," "You are the salt of the earth,"* he told the peasant multitudes in Israel. He spoke like He was convinced His hearers could *actually do* the remarkable things He taught them.

4 R. J. STAUB

Avoiding religious language, He used the most common themes of family, and work, and commerce to frame His appeal for wholesome and godly living. His teachings about the kingdom of God easily found their expression through the everyday activities of life. That is precisely *the gospel*; Jesus has brought the kingdom of God near so that every individual may participate truly and fully in His purposeful redemptive activity.

A journey of discovery

For twenty centuries the events surrounding the life of Jesus of Nazareth, and men's beliefs about what they mean, have generated perhaps the most widely diverse collection of religious practices under a single name, *Christianity*, in all of history. The recorded teachings of Jesus are interpreted and implemented in almost every conceivable way, from the primitive and superstitious to the sophisticated, culturally sensitive imaginings of 21st century marketing.

As I've tried to clearly comprehend Jesus' teachings, and present them in the simplest, most understandable terms I can muster, I've frequently found myself confounded by some widely accepted ideas, traditions, and even institutions within American Christianity. At the same time, years of Christian service have brought my wife Jeanie and me in contact with thousands of believers and ministry folk, and in many of them I've observed a very preconceived, stereotypical, and culturally-directed concept of what Jesus intended for His disciples, and for those of us who have come after. We'll look at the reasons for that and its impact.

Though many have attempted through the centuries to set down an order or arrangement for Christian doctrine and practice, none has emerged as definitive for more than a small cross section of the churches. In reality, that is quite understandable since Jesus

Himself had little to say about how his legacy should be observed. In fact, His most outstanding request was that whenever believers sit down to a meal together, they pause to remember His love and provision for them. (1 Cor. 11:23-26) So, the fact that folks practice their commitment to Jesus Christ in a myriad of ways is no surprise. What *is* surprising, however, is how critical and intolerant many of them are about how others do it.

Professing Christians are often confused by the many conflicting representations of the church, all claiming the better understanding and interpretation of Jesus' message. From baptism to infant dedications, from conversion to confirmation, from store front churches to grand cathedrals, from speaking in tongues to vows of silence or poverty; the variations in custom, doctrine, and practice are dizzying.

On top of that, American Christianity is a massive institutional entity; complex, sectarian, competitive, and cumbersome, often getting in its own way. It has an imposing presence in the society, but its impact, both spiritual and cultural, is diminishing. There is abundant statistical support for this (churches closing 4 to 1 over new ones beginning, declining attendance in most groups, and a rapidly growing non-Christian share of the population) but most significant, however, is the sad fact that morally, ethically, and in terms of overall values, the statistical difference between the choices and behaviors of professing Christians and those of non-Christians is often barely distinguishable. So, it's not surprising that the unbelieving world usually catalogues organized Christianity as just another socio/economic enterprise. The abundance of endeavor in the *name* of Christ has frequently become an impediment to actually understanding and experiencing Christ Himself.

Finally, in reading the gospels it doesn't take long before we realize *there is little need for clergy or catechism, for denomination or doctrine, for organization or a building for a believer to do the words in red.* Paul instructed Timothy to teach those same words, *"wholesome words, even the words of our Lord Jesus Christ."* (1 Timothy 6:3)

However, as we go forward we'll discuss how clergy, doctrine, and organization may be a significant support and encouragement in a believer's life. But it is of vital importance that men and women who are 'born of the Spirit' (John 3:3-7) understand the proper role and function of what most folks call 'church.'

We begin by recognizing that Jesus didn't provide a strict, prescriptive form for living as His disciples, and therefore it's up to us to pay careful attention to His words and His example, ordering our lives after them. At the same time, we must decide if Christianity as an American cultural institution faithfully represents Jesus' interests, and if it effectively communicates the substance and Spirit which is Jesus Christ Himself. It is our purpose to discover for ourselves and our families the very simple and personal nature of Jesus' invitation to *'follow Me.'*

2

RETIRING A MYTH

Every religion has its myths, including Christianity. They're
not usually sinister, they're just misleading. One such myth in
Christianity is; *"God has a wonderful plan for your life!"* * This promise is repeated ritually in churches, gospel crusades, prayer groups;
anywhere Christians are encouraging others to follow Jesus. It is
declared with sincerity and conviction as an incentive toward a
'decision for Christ.' By embracing the 'wonderful plan' idea, one
might find the uncertainties of the future moderated to some degree by the prospect of a divinely conceived agenda for one's life.

However, even as a young person I was troubled by that statement. As reasonable and inviting as it sounds, the fact is, *no one
knows* what specific plan God has for his life, or for *anyone's* life for
that matter, and if God actually has one, it's not something we can
discuss with any real certainty. Although most believers enjoy a
sense of purpose or direction regarding their future, people rarely
experience life unfolding in precisely the way they had anticipated.

Since the 'wonderful plan for your life' is not really spelled
out anywhere for an individual, many believers find themselves

grappling with a puzzle they can't solve, a mystery difficult to un-
ravel, or a necessary revelation they somehow missed, particularly
when life inevitably takes a turn or two away from their expectations. Years into the journey many faithful Christians become
disillusioned because they think they've never really 'landed on
it.' The 'wonderful plan' remains elusive, mysterious, and frustrat-
ingly obscure. And sometimes the weight of life and its considerable hardships cause these good folk to become weary with it all,
and conclude that they were misled or they're somehow spiritually
inferior.

Often the poets deal with the tough stuff that regular folks
avoid. I remember first hearing this lament in Paul Simon's 1977
billboard hit, "Slip Slidin' Away."

> 'God only knows; God makes His plan
> The information's unavailable to the mortal man
> We're working our jobs, collect our pay
> Believe we're gliding down the highway
> When in fact we're slip slidin' away.'

This song exposes the terrible dilemma of having hope in some
divine purpose for one's life but at the same time fearing it has
somehow eluded us; slipped from our grasp. It's tough to hear the
disillusionment of folks dealing with that dread.

Some will quickly point out that the Bible contains the plan of
God for our lives, and in a general sense that is so. The scriptures
unveil redemption; God's rescue of humanity from the awful ef-
fects of sin and guilt through the death of Christ. Every Christian
group explains how this works a bit differently, but they have that
in common. After we are converted, we are encouraged by the
scriptures to engage God through prayer, the Bible, fellowshipping

with other believers, and to live in confidence that life has an order to it that God somehow directs.

However, the information that is still 'unavailable' is that particular or unique plan that God may have for *your life; your predetermined assignment.* That seems to be the thorny part of this 'wonderful plan of God' business. Even if God were to reveal such a plan, you might not find it all that comforting. Consider His 'wonderful plan' for Saul of Tarsus; *"I will show (you) how many things (you) must suffer for My name's sake."* (Acts 9:16) Not an exciting send-off for a new believer!

Of course, depending on the particular stream of Christianity one grows up in, or is introduced to upon conversion, knowing God's plan may or may not be any kind of issue. Many Christian traditions entertain the 'absentee landlord' concept of God; He owns all the stuff but you can pretty much do with it what you want, and as long as you don't do anything gross, it will be okay with Him. In other words, there are no *particulars* to living the Christian life, only generalities. God is not in the details (*even if the devil is*); He doesn't micromanage human beings, even if they'd like Him to. Any 'plan of God' is His business alone.

Other folks, however, have a different set of expectations for their Christian journey. They're taught to expect specific answers to specific prayers; *that 'whatever you ask when you pray, believe that you receive it and you will have it.'* They believe God has in mind particular events, encounters, challenges, assignments, and outcomes for their lives, and they're obliged to be looking for distinct clues, signs, or words that will engage them with 'the will of God.'

So, it's easy to see that the level of one's expectations will likely have a direct bearing on one's potential for frustration or disappointment. It's important, then, to come to some kind of resolution about this matter of God's 'wonderful plan for your life,' and what the actual reality is. In challenging a cherished idea, I realize in all likelihood some people will prefer the myth. I celebrate everyone's freedom.

The fact is, there's no mystery to God's plan for your life. **You are the Plan**. God's purposes for you are realized *in this very precious and unique moment*, not in some forecast for the future. Moses clarified God's perspective on this issue 40 centuries ago, echoed by Paul in his letter to the Romans; *". . . . it is not too mysterious for you, nor is it far off. . . . but the word is very near you, in your mouth and in your heart, that you may do it."* (Deut. 30:11, 14; Romans 10:9) As we will find out, that's the gospel truth!

---

*I use the term 'myth' in its secondary meaning: *'a popular belief or tradition that has grown up around something . . . one embodying the ideals of a segment of society.'* – Webster's New Collegiate

3

THE CHRISTIAN LANDSCAPE

She caught our attention immediately. Seated near the front in the congregation of 400 was a very elderly woman smiling widely and intermittently weeping. No one near her seemed to notice, and this was not the first time. In a couple of previous meetings her presentation was the same. Jeanie and I were curious.

It was the winter of 1995 in a city in Western Russia. We had joined a couple of good friends, seasoned missionaries, for a couple weeks of ministry in, and out from, a wonderful church started not long after the collapse of the Soviet Union. After the Sunday morning service concluded we asked the pastor about the beaming, weeping woman we had observed. "Ah, Maya!" he laughed. "Yes, she does that through every worship meeting!"

He went on to explain that she had become a believer as a young girl, near the time of the Russian revolution. Several of her family had been converted by reading parts of the Bible, particularly the Book of Acts. For 8 decades they had been part of the hidden church in Russia. All those years Maya had prayed for a time when the believers she knew could be free to experience the joy of open worship and fellowship she read about in the Bible. Her tears were those of gratitude and fulfillment.

What has lingered with us in the years since was the depth of one woman's desire to see her personal reality mirror what is seen in the scriptures. And perhaps her prayer may represent a desire in *all* true believers. *Is it possible to experience the things we see in the Bible?* Not those singular events, of course, like the parting of the Red Sea, or the mount of transfiguration, but rather the vibrant environment surrounding Pentecost, and the joy, generosity, and dynamic influence of the saints in the season following it? Or the conversion and Spirit baptism of Cornelius' entire household? Or the disciples becoming known as 'Christians' at Antioch, along with the healings, the deliverances, the miraculous provisions, the deep sense of community, and the gatherings of the early church leaders which promoted liberty rather than sectarian division?

Believers in every era are encouraged and fortified when their own experience sometimes becomes, in observable ways, reflective of the biblical record. I've wondered if this desire in us helps explain the 'veneration of saints' within some Christian traditions; a strong identification with believers who experienced powerful encounters with God throughout the church's history.

The American Church

To help us with this inquiry, let's begin by looking at the various forms of Christianity as they are practiced in American society. It is not possible in this brief context (nor am I qualified) to speak with any clarity about Christianity around the world. Since the United States is perhaps the most fertile ground for observing 'creative' Christian endeavor, we'll limit our scrutiny to the forms of the faith we see around us, hopefully with both charity and candor. We'll compare the mainstream movements (traditional, evangelical, Pentecostal/charismatic, reformed, Catholic, etc.) and some of their distinctive characteristics with the biblical / apostolic examples. It's important to recognize their contributions as well as identifying their limitations. Of course, for our rather compact analysis these observations will largely be generalities, and exceptions are noted.

Evaluating American Christianity for American readers is challenging precisely because in many people's minds we are, or were, or should be a Christian society, something the nation's Founders clearly intended to avoid. That many of them were Christians is incidental to the greater fact that they wanted for everyone a guarantee of *freedom* in matters of worship. Also, there are quite a number of American Christians who view democratic capitalism as God's 'approved' form for societal development.

I mention this because the tendency within the church to blend Christianity with American culture makes it difficult for many people to grasp the profoundly *different* mind-set of the kingdom of God. Despite the activist disposition of many sincere believers, God isn't competing for a place at the socio/political table in this culture or any other. Color Him neither *red* nor *blue*. God is calling and creating individuals who understand the need for redemption on a personal level (1 Cor. 5:17), and who are willing to carry forward the radical message of His transforming love through Jesus Christ into a culture quite oblivious to, or perhaps content with, its hypocrisies, greed, racism, and violence.

Sadly, Institutional Christianity, and many professing Christians, often fail to present a life paradigm significantly different from modern culture; thus their witness to Jesus is quite distorted or, at the least, diluted. In the past few years, **Barna Research Group** has polled thousands of churches and clergy, and tens of thousands of 'professing' Christians and 'born again' Christians. The result shows a disturbing disconnect between what Christians profess to believe and (1) what their leaders *actually preach,* and (2) how their professed beliefs impact their choices and behaviors.

For example, among churches polled, just 28% believe the Bible is inspired and authoritative. 90% of clergymen simply don't teach on the difficult moral, ethical, and behavioral questions facing believers today. Two-thirds of Christians admit to lying pretty regularly, and about 80% believe other religions also show the sincere individual a way to heaven. A mere 20% of 'born again' Christians believe in any absolute truth, that Satan is real, that Jesus was sinless, or that God rules the world. The incident of divorce, premarital sex, homosexuality, or looking to psychic sources for guidance is about the same among Christians as non-Christians. Of the Christians polled, fully one-third feel church isn't relevant to their daily life in any way.

It is evident there remains a great need for men and women who take seriously the words of scripture; who take *personal responsibility* for living by them, and who embrace the challenge of helping create a community that exemplifies them . . . . the *'witness'* Jesus asked for. (Acts 1:8)

American Christianity is also remarkably diverse, with an entire constellation of subgroups surrounding the major denominations and traditions. How this came to be is described in a practical way by Catholic author Henri Nouwen in his essay, The Prayer of the Heart:

> *"The spiritual wisdom of many Christians, who in the course of history have dedicated their lives to prayer, is preserved and relived in the different traditions, life styles, or spiritualties that remain visible in contemporary Christianity. In fact, our first and most influential guides are often the prayer customs, styles of worship and modes of speaking about God that pervade our different milieu.*

Each spiritual milieu has its own emphasis. Here silence is stressed, there study of the scriptures; here individual meditation is central, there communal worship; here poverty is the unifying concept, there it is obedience; here the great mystical experiences are suggested as the way to perfection, there the little way of common daily life. Much of the emphasis depends on the time in which a new spirituality found its beginning, on the personal character of the man or woman who was or is its main inspiration, and on the particular needs to which it responds." (Reaching out; HJM Nouwen, 1986)

All of the ministries, or 'spiritualties' as Father Nouwen calls them, had their genesis in a particular place and time, and represent the efforts of men or women trying to meet what they considered a particular need in the Christian community. They organize and build churches, create mission organizations, form home groups, establish denominations, etc. The scriptures give them the right to do that. But it also makes them responsible for whether or not their efforts support God's priorities. (1 Corinthians 3:9-13; James 3:1) The recognition of this fact, and what it implies, is most important to this discussion.

The varying forms of worship within Christianity are not at issue here. One may personally approach God in many ways; in quietness and solitude, by prayer and confession, by liturgy and sacrament, or in praise and adoration. The only consistent requisite is that we come to God **in faith** *(". . . he that comes to God must believe that He is, and that He is a rewarder of those who diligently seek Him."* Heb. 11:6) and **through the Mediator,** *"the man Christ Jesus."* (1 Tim. 2:5)

So, I pose a question which I first asked myself decades ago: *Does the complex organizational / institutional model of the*

church so dominant in America represent and offer what Jesus had in mind when he spoke of life in the kingdom of God?
This immediately calls in question the foundations of institutional Christianity on very practical, as well as scriptural grounds. Again, the need for *organization* in any corporate enterprise is obvious, so to be clear, when we speak of 'institutional Christianity' we're referring to those groups that have systematized their doctrine and practice, and perhaps even their dress, manner, and vocabulary. Deviation from the prescribed norms by its participants constitutes a compromise, and may call in question the orthodoxy, or even the salvation of the transgressor. How strenuously these distinguishing markers are applied and enforced varies from group to group, but there is a strong *tendency* by highly structured Christian endeavors to be rigid, exclusive, and self-affirming, and over time their religious system is fixed, packaged, and franchised, thereby constituting what may be called *Institutional Christianity.*

It is important to make a distinction between Institutional / denominational Christianity and the thousands of independent or non-affiliated fellowships throughout our culture. Both, of course, are accountable to the Lord for their efforts, that they serve kingdom interests; something we will shortly discuss in some detail. However, many of the independent churches have not systematized their forms and doctrines, and therefore are frequently less rigid in their interaction with the saints and other traditions, and able to be more responsive to both, and to God's Spirit.

Also, many of the men and women who serve these congregations are not bound to the constraints placed on clergymen by denominational Christianity, which may include a weighty constitution and bylaws, doctrinal imperatives, operational guidelines, ministerial protocols, career tracks, financial obligations, and the strict oversight of a hierarchy of some kind. Of course, independent groups face other challenges that are uniquely their own, as there will be pitfalls in any enterprise involving a mixture of people, religion, authority, and money.

For our purpose, let's simply note the fact that there are an almost infinite variety of forms and practices churches may adopt, but those which are unencumbered by a highly developed religious structure *may* be less prone to some of the weaknesses, insensitivities, and abuses that afflict many Christian institutions.

Who represents God?

To the point . . . . While Institutional Christianity is not *wrong*, there may not be anything inherently *right* about it either. It just is what is. Christian folks participate because it's mostly what has been constructed around them and offered to them. And further, the organized church, in all its many forms, has no *intrinsic* right to be regarded as the God-ordained representative of His kingdom. Although it is obvious that Institutional Christianity *expects* the saints, and indeed the surrounding community, to regard it as exactly that, there is no biblical basis for it.

Precisely who confers that distinction on a religious institution? Has *God* authorized Catholicism, or Adventism, or the Assemblies of God, or the Southern Baptist Convention, or the Episcopal Church in America to officially represent His kingdom? No, He hasn't. These are all man-made entities, created to represent and promote someone's view of corporate Christianity, and how it should best be configured and function.

Having said that, does it also imply that the individuals carrying out these works are not worthy of our respect and recognition? Of course not. Let's assume that many, perhaps most of those souls are truly converted believers, and thus our brothers and sisters in Christ. We should afford them the regard, and indeed the authority that is commensurate with the Spirit of God that lives and works through them. In evaluating the institutional church's functions, we must necessarily discern those edicts and actions that have a biblical basis, or issue from the Holy Spirit, or from wisdom and experience, distinguishable from those that serve only the interests and agenda of the organization. This is not black or white; there are indeed gray areas, just as there are in our interaction with government, business, or the arts.

Obviously, it is easy to criticize. In this discussion we are careful to distinguish between the nature and role of religious institutions and the integrity or motives of people. *This commentary is not directed toward any person or group.* I am blessed to call 'my friends' many of the good and godly men and women who function commendably within the organized church. Their good service, however, does not earn a divine endorsement for a particular organizational structure or worship form. A gracious God works with us in whatever context we create for Him.

It has been interesting to watch the recent selection of Pope Francis. It is a challenge to even contemplate the vast structures of Catholicism, both physical and ecclesiastical, and try to grasp how the process of papal transition actually impacts the rank and file Catholic in any truly significant way. The monumental reforms that challenge the new pontiff are stark testimony to the impersonal, thoroughly secular, and crushingly insensitive nature of most institutions, religious or otherwise.

In contrast, his predecessor, Pope Benedict XVI, in his early years as a priest and theologian, envisioned the church of the future. He saw it functioning *outside* the great Cathedrals, composed of smaller groups led by lay-people, not clergymen. A kind of 'home-grown' Catholicism, centered in personal devotion and relationships. *"Contrary to what has happened until now, (the church) will present herself much more as a community of volunteers . . . as a small community, she will demand much more from the initiative of each of her members and she will certainly also acknowledge new forms of ministry,*

and will raise up to the priesthood proven Christians who will have other jobs . . ."
That vision has surfaced again and again through the years in almost
every branch of the church.

I was barely out of my teens when I first encountered the insensitive, impersonal characteristics of a religious hierarchy; in this case,
an organization our families had loyally supported for decades. I was
making application for a ministerial license, but regrettably I was attending a church which had recently moved outside of their organizational sanction, choosing to not require attendees to become 'official'
members before they could vote. The organization didn't approve of
me fellowshipping with those folks, even though my church's basic
beliefs and practice were virtually identical to their own.

My relative youth made the discussion and outcome pretty
one-sided. It was obvious, to them at least, that my inexperience
with 'how things work' far outweighed my appeal for a reasonable
dialogue about their position. Of course I was immensely disappointed, but over time I realized it all had little to do with me personally. I was nobody. I had simply met 'the system' within that
particular group and it had applied its template, and spit me out.
Nothing personal; *'Please go away, and God bless you as you go.'*

The ensuing 50 years have brought me a lot of valuable perspective about organized Christianity, and Jeanie and I were privileged
to pastor a non-denominational church for almost twenty-three
of those years. I've retained my appreciation and affection for the
organization that passed on me (thankfully, not *everyone* did!), and
more importantly for the many good souls within it who invested
in my early life. Most of those folks had good hearts and honorable intentions, and had little idea of the frequent craziness issuing
from their regional headquarters.

So again, there is virtually nothing in the words of Jesus or
the Apostles that suggests what we have today; an infinite variety

of organizations, denominations (over 25,000 worldwide), and church complexes, each with its own hierarchies, structures, moral and spiritual codes, language, heroes and superstars, career tracks, and a prescribed public persona. Now, one might argue that the huge increase in world population in 2000 years would necessarily demand a corresponding organizational model to facilitate the interaction of larger numbers of believers. That's a legitimate observation, so the challenge before us is to evaluate whether or not the existing organizations / institutions are faithfully carrying out the kingdom directives of Jesus Christ. If so, and to whatever degree, God bless and prosper them. If not, then neither the strength nor grandeur of their cultural presence, nor the scope or sophistication of their operation is at all meaningful to the kingdom of God.

Religious Systems

Institutional Christianity, by its nature, seizes on the energies, talents, gifts, time, and resources of the saints, using them to support and expand its religious structure. It purports to be the gatekeeper for the service of God, for meaningful relationships, and for the kingdom's resources, and by its very presence in the community it hopes to command recognition and respect.

A large segment of these institutions develop on the premise that the assembly, or corporate gathering, is the 'center,' and thus everything is configured to enlarge it. This is not always taught, it is assumed. Much of the perceived success of the work, and consequently its cultural and denominational influence, is determined by how large the assembly becomes. With that population as its base, virtually every activity, from the Sacraments to the softball team, is driven and sanctioned by the organization and its hierarchies. This highly developed and visible structure promotes in many saints a sense of obligation to it simply because it exists 'in Jesus name.' Religion always makes a strong case for its necessary rights and privileges.

In an address to the faculty and staff at Southern Cal, skateboarding legend Rodney Mullen described how *'context shapes content'* as modern street skaters explore new vistas for their sport. As I listened to his remarks I realized how this axiom is clearly applicable to the organized church. The institutional context inevitably shapes the content of the mission and message, skewing it to one degree or another toward being increasingly self-serving, authoritarian, and sectarian. Channeling most charitable giving and service through the institution, requiring rigorous, mandatory indoctrination for 'membership,' and limiting corporate fellowship to groups of like doctrine and practice are just a few examples.

Further, religious structures have a very limited ability to respond positively to the individuality, creativity, inspiration, and uniqueness that God's Spirit produces in His saints. While institutions particularly value conformity and compliance, God treasures those singular characteristics in each of us that glorify His ongoing artistry on the human canvas. As Christian institutions grow the resulting tension between creativity and conformity heightens, except in the case of the exceptionally gifted. They usually find their way onto the platform.

The priorities of religious organizations are usually in direct correlation to the spiritual understanding and sensitivity of the individuals functioning within them, and certainly God's people have done some splendid things in the institutional church setting. However, in many cases there is a watershed at which the religious structure begins to command more service (time, money, energy, and recognition) than the people it was created to serve (though few leaders have the courage to identify it). The multitude of facilities, projects, groups, activities, social services, and entertainments in 'full-service' Christianity sometimes impose themselves in direct competition with the priorities of the kingdom. Please consider the prophetic wisdom of author Laurie Beth Jones; *"What God can bless as a **supplement** He must curse as a **substitute**."* (L. B. J., Jesus: CEO)

Complicating this issue further is the money-driven nature of many church institutions. Large budgets, sometimes multi-million dollar budgets, supporting a sizable facility or even one or more extensive campuses, necessarily require a business model which will significantly shape the priorities and policies of the organization. This of course is managed, not by people of the Spirit (exceptions are indeed rare), but by a board of directors, or something akin to it. This is a sensitive area, full of pitfalls and peril. Let me simply say I have a great deal of sympathy for leaders who are caught in that terrible contest, as two gods are vying for the same throne in the churches. (Matthew 6:24, Rev. 3:17-19) Mammon almost always gains the advantage; the living God does not compete.

Again, let's be very clear. Institutional, cultural Christianity, as it is visible on the street corners and in the suburbs of our cities, is entirely man made. In fact, much of it is interfaced with 'the world;' a realm we must interact with cautiously. (1 John 2:15-17) Now to say something is man-made is not to say it is wrong, or that it shouldn't exist. But for complete clarity within this discussion, it's very important to identify its origins.

'Man made' simply means that the organizational structure, forms, and practices of the institutional church are based on someone's religious or biblical perspectives and preferences. The stated mission of the work, its priorities, and criteria for participation are, to one degree or another, set by its organizers. This may all be done sincerely and prayerfully, and for that reason we view it respectfully, but in the final analysis, its spiritual value and kingdom significance rests entirely upon its *actual impact* on the inner life and practice of the saints, and its passion for true worship and the glory of God.

The fact is, one can find membership, fellowship, personal affirmation, support groups, community service, helpful information, and a good cup of coffee in hundreds of places, but *the church of Jesus Christ is the place one goes to experience what cannot be found anywhere else.*

Folks may argue that the organizations and forms that have been created are God ordained, and those who created them were instructed by God to do so. The fact is, no one knows if that is so or not; God owns all such insights. The best we can do is look at the godly influence of these organizations; that is, to what extent do they promote life in the Spirit among those serving, and those served by them (Romans 14:17), and carry out the commands of Jesus concerning the society around them? However, *this* we can say with certainty; institutions don't know anyone, feel anything, or care about anything. They're only tools. When they fail to help us prioritize and produce the desired result, the thing that is in the heart of God for *people*, we must change them or abandon them. The King doesn't waste anything or anyone.

It is surely curious that so many Christian groups, particularly the evangelicals, fiercely defend their commitment to being biblical, yet have so little Bible foundation for much of their institutional form and practice. *Biblically*, a church is not a building or a business, 'pastor' is not a CEO, president, or a 'life coach,' deacons or committees don't 'hire' pastors, worship isn't just a sampling of 'up-tempo' contemporary praise music, and the saints aren't required to finance a religious enterprise just because it calls itself a church.

The fact is, we *have no biblical or practical obligation to organized Christianity.* Believers may participate and support these organizations if they choose to, and in many cases those saints are the better for it. But, much like circumcision practiced among the early Jewish believers, affiliation is irrelevant to one's standing with God.

Again, we *are* obligated to the faithful men and women within the organized church, to speak well of them, and value their service. But the entrepreneurs, the vocational clergymen, the opportunists, the manipulators, money changers, seducers, and false prophets populating and propelling some of these institutions? We have no obligation to them, even if they do occupy the 'best seats in the synagogues' (Matt. 23:6).

Precisely because there is this kind of mixture (people, policies, and priorities) in the organized church, there are well documented abuses, exploitations, and personal tragedies throughout her history. We might expect as much, and not be shocked by it, when we acknowledge these church institutions are created by people. And because they are, those responsible cannot opt out of accountability for these abuses by claiming the institution is God given and stands on its own by divine right. No, someone created it, and they, or their successors, are answerable for it.

"We have what you need!"

Institutional Christianity often falls short in her obligation to be honest with the client, something one would expect any reputable enterprise to be. Those offering goods or services must make clear to the consumer the things they may reasonably expect from the product or service and the limitations of it. It may be in 'fine print' but it is disclosed nonetheless. I recall telling my congregation numerous times, *"Ninety percent of what you'll need to live the Christian life you must pursue and obtain for yourself; you'll only get a sampling here."* That statement was never followed by applause; I suspect relatively few saints took it to heart.

"Full service" Christianity often represents itself as a relatively complete prescription for the spiritual health of the entire family. This claim is made in varying degrees from group to group. While this may be an attractive concept, in truth it is wholly unrealistic and unattainable. It suggests the kingdom of God is like a carnival, and the local church-house the midway, with attractions galore, bright lights, food, entertainment, and skilled barkers coaxing the celebrants into the right doorway. Everyone goes home thoroughly stimulated; filled up with good stuff. This is clearly visible, particularly among some larger congregations and mega-churches. This representation is suggested / implied in media, materials, and in the public gatherings: *"We have what you need."*

The fact is, institutional Christianity can provide only a small part of what believers need to have a robust life of faith in Christ. Packaging, however, can make everything 'appear' very substantive, through pomp and ceremony, through lights and sound, through events and activities, and through some carefully calibrated *pieces* of the gospel message that appeal to basic human needs and wants. There was a reason that the crowds moved *away* from Jesus Christ from time to time. He represented precisely what following Him required, and the cost involved in full participation. That's why so many folks choose to 'dabble' in the faith just enough to borrow the label 'Christian.'

Over lunch one day several years ago, a colleague and I asked Bob Willhite, then director of the Prayer Embassy in Washington D.C., what was happening in the churches he was ministering in around the country. *"Mostly they're doing everything they can to keep people in the pews until God moves again!"* Big budgets and 21st century amenities demand lots of people participating and giving money, no matter what it takes.

In the public consciousness religious institutions are sometimes awarded a 'persona' of sorts, which leads some people to put a certain amount of trust in them. The expectation is that the organization has character, integrity, and a view toward their best interests. That idea can lead to real disappointment when the people working within the organization don't reflect the ideals that are attributed to that group. For this reason discriminating believers should be careful who or what they identify with, and who they allow to represent them.

It's important to distinguish between 'value' and 'virtue' when looking at Christian institutions. They may indeed be valuable when they are being used to serve kingdom purposes, but there is nothing at all virtuous, or spiritual, or moral about an organization. Only people, through their attitudes and actions, can display these things. Nevertheless, the institutional church often represents itself as an essential catalyst, either directly or in the sense of oversight, in almost all legitimate kingdom transactions, thereby giving them sanction and credibility. And when people assign this authority to a religious institution, in some cases they will allow that system to think for them, represent them, repress them, threaten them, condemn them, and make them pay money for it. Not a good deal.

We must also carefully distinguish between intent and result. I'm not suggesting that the decision-makers in the churches deliberately misinform people. The fact is, however, many churchmen function on the presupposition that organized Christianity evolved by a divine design or sanction, and based on that assumption they teach that without a visible, structured church system to support them, believers cannot be faithful, fruitful Christians.

That, however, is not so. Later we'll be suggesting what the healthy role of church institutions might be, and how the saints may engage them for mutual benefit and blessing.

Now, this whole discussion may seem rather sophomoric unless one firmly acknowledges two things. First, how thorough, complete, and far-reaching regeneration through faith in Jesus Christ really is, and how very much confidence God has in *every one* of His saints. God's resource is His people; *all of them!* Sadly, in too many cases that great truth is denied the people in the pews as they are unwittingly *trained* to obediently sit, listen, nod, and fetch.

Jesus taught that His kingdom 'is not of this world;' it is not visible in the ordinary sense, and its holy headquarters is within the heart of the men and women who follow Him. *"Your body is God's temple,"* Paul taught. In fact, the book of Hebrews completely dismantles the notion that we have any continuing obligation to formalized religion, governed by rules and a priesthood. Christ completely fulfilled all the demands of the law for us, and embraced us in a relationship so intimate there remains little need for any *religion* at all!

"For this is the covenant that I will make with the house of Israel after those days, says the Lord: I will put My laws in their mind and write them on their hearts; and I will be their God, and they shall be My people. None of them shall teach his neighbor, and none his brother, saying, 'know the Lord,' for all shall know Me, from the least of them to the greatest of them. For I shall be merciful to their unrighteousness, and their sins and their lawless deeds I will remember no more." (Heb. 8:10-12; Jer. 31:33, 34 - ref: Heb. 8:1-9, 13)

In saying this, however, we all realize that the church as a community of believers must necessarily take *some* kind of shape or form in every social context. Christians, like any group, are going to congregate, celebrate, discuss stuff, and eat food. In order to do that some organization, coordination, leadership, and a roof and kitchen are required. The particular *form* their gatherings take will be at the discretion of well-meaning people, configured in a multitude of ways, in a variety of places. Jeanie and I have celebrated Jesus with believers in churches of every description, and also in homes, storefronts, offices, civic centers, tents, campgrounds, parks, and the city dump. They were all a joyous opportunity to share the gospel of God, and entertain His presence.

The vital element within any Christian assembly, however, is that its primary function is to serve the interests of Jesus in the lives of the participants. What *are* His interests exactly? That each believer might become a *functioning part* of the Kingdom of God. Jesus suffered and died that men and women might be regenerated (born again), filled with His Spirit, and equipped, energized, and liberated to live joyfully and purposefully in fellowship with Him. The main agenda of any Christian endeavor, then, should be to facilitate those things in any way possible, and that requires saints and leaders who understand the priorities and principles of His kingdom, something we'll be discussing in the next chapter.

These observations do not imply that saints who feel more comfortable within institutional Christianity are somehow ill informed, or less spiritual than those who serve the Lord in a different context. Let's wisely avoid creating another religious caste-system. Remember, this analysis is about the nature of religious institutions, not about the relative spiritual depth of the individuals functioning in or outside them. Most generally, that insight is not accessible to us . . . . nor should it be. (Matt. 7:1-5)

Institutional Christianity is here to stay; indeed, some believers will not feel comfortable, or spiritual, or even *safe* without it. That's understandable. For some, form or tradition will not be traded for any perceived freedom or added function. Every saint has the right to choose. Many of the early Jewish Christians, for example, kept the forms and traditions of Judaism through much of the first century, because it was an integral and cherished part of their culture and daily routine.

However, in 1999 I heard the Lord speak in my heart; *"The present forms of American Christianity will not adequately serve the 21st century."* Now, nearly two decades into that period, informed observers tell us that increasing numbers of seekers, particularly the younger ones, are choosing to pursue a relationship with Jesus Christ *outside* the institutional church. Coupled with that, a recent survey documented that 70% of Christian young people are leaving the organized church after a year in college. Rather than viewing this negatively, perhaps it is an opportunity to explore new venues for Christian fellowship and endeavor. When the saints are 'on the move' it may signal that God is going before them. It's happened before. (Ex. 40:34-38)

It is important for all the saints, regardless of where they have chosen to serve the Lord, to remember this great truth; *the Holy Spirit promotes unity rather than division.* We should always be open, and welcome opportunities to engage and support the kingdom activities of believers in every context. Speaking practically, organized Christianity makes possible large corporate gatherings, conferences, Bible schools, etc.; all requiring some substantial facilities and oversight. So, there is an obvious benefit to the saints inherent in the church's institutions.

At the same time, we should awaken to the present need for a prayerful reconsideration of the words of Jesus and the apostolic examples. We must never stop learning and growing, enabling us, by God's grace, to make a positive contribution to kingdom understanding and function during our brief moments on the time-line.

4

THE CHURCH AND THE KINGDOM

> The organized church is truthful, purposeful, and
> dynamic in direct proportion to how faithfully the
> individuals within the church are responsive to the
> Kingdom.

The New Testament introduces the ministry of Jesus Christ; *"From
that time Jesus began to preach and to say, 'Repent, for the **kingdom of
heaven** is at hand (has drawn near).'"* (Matt. 4:17) After His resurrection, Jesus spent 40 days with His men, *"speaking of the things
pertaining to the **kingdom of God**."* (Acts 1:3) Decades later, Luke
concludes his brief church history with the aged Paul in Rome,
*"preaching the **kingdom of God** and teaching the things which concern the
Lord Jesus Christ."* (Acts 28:31)

From beginning to end, Jesus' gospel focused on the kingdom
of God (Daniel 2:44) and how men and women might enter it,
and function within it. At the same time, He offered no known
instruction for creating religious structures to facilitate spiritual
life and practice. Consequently, to advocate for the integrity of the

scriptures, let's look again at the kingdom of God and its relation to the American Christian complex.

One of the disturbing things I encounter in visiting with many Christians is their perception of themselves in relation to the imposing volume of church organizations and institutions present in our society. Many seem to feel like a tiny figure living in the lengthy shadow of these religious entities which constitute, in their minds, the domain of God. Their obligation is to somehow find the right door to get inside and subsequently do their part to further its holy existence. It is an intimidation of sorts that, in most cases, is unintended but is nonetheless created and perpetuated by the significant cultural presence of organized Christianity.

The *perception* is that this great religious complex is ordained by God, and is operated by folks who are likely more capable and spiritual than regular people. The church's structures, forms, and rituals promote the conviction that they are somehow patterned after a heavenly archetype, and one's participation with them assures one of divine acceptance and eventual absolution.

The fact is, Christian institutions are indeed *the shadow*, and not the thing of substance. Again, one has only to read the book of Hebrews to see how God, through the life, death, and resurrection of Jesus Christ, essentially brought to a conclusion the holy purpose of ceremonial Judaism, and set out an entirely new way to approach God which makes much formal religious practice appear tedious, and to some degree, irrelevant.

As a starting place, please consider the following general characteristics of the kingdom of God compared to the church. In this illustration, we are using the term 'church' as our culture uses it, referring to the religious presence called Christianity (Institutions, organizations, denominations, buildings, etc.). As we stated before, in scripture 'church' means *people*.

The Kingdom of God	The Organized Church
Invisible	Visible
Heavenly	Earthly
Eternal	Temporal
Infinite	Finite
Unchanging	Changing
Reigning	Battling
Incorruptible	Corruptible
Administered by the Spirit	Administered by men

Kingdom Orientation

"If you have not chosen the kingdom of God first, it will in the end make no difference what you've chosen instead."

—William Law

When we speak of kingdom orientation, or of developing a kingdom perspective, we are speaking about relating to God and His realm; something that will, before anything else, require in every person a spiritual transformation. *"Unless one is born again he cannot see the kingdom of God."* (John 3:3) To the un-regenerated person, the spiritual realm is a fantasy; it makes no sense to him. Engagement with that realm demands revelation and faith, both of which come by a divine transaction; a gift of God through our response to the gospel. The five senses and one's rationale cannot open this door. The kingdom of God is founded on different principles (holiness, obedience, character) and does business by a different currency (love, mercy, forgiveness, truth) than the systems of government and commerce we relate to in daily life.

Consequently, the world of church buildings, denominations, ministry organizations, creeds, and doctrines, which is known culturally as Christianity, is merely suggestive of more substantive and enduring realities which are part of the spiritual realm, but which deeply impact our lives. Paul stated this in the plainest language; *"We do not look at the things which are seen, but at the things which are not seen. For the things which are seen are temporary, but the things which are not seen are eternal."* (2 Cor. 4:18)

All *visible* Christian endeavor (churches, denominations, etc.) within a society, then, is organized and constructed utilizing someone's understanding (or misunderstanding) of God's kingdom. So in order to fairly evaluate what we call 'Christianity' around us, we must get a firm grasp on the distinctive qualities of the kingdom of God, and how believers are to interact with it.

Jesus had little to say about 'church.' *"I will build my church, and the gates of hell shall not prevail against it."* Other than this reference (and one about church discipline), Jesus spoke exclusively of the Kingdom. Judaism, which is not only a faith but also a *family*, wasn't at all suited for the nature and scope of His mission. *"Seek first the Kingdom of God, and His righteousness . . . ,"* He told the crowds on the hillside. Throughout His earthly ministry Jesus stressed the need for every person to understand and vigorously grasp hold of His Kingdom. (Matt. 11:12)

A fundamental kingdom scripture is Luke 17:20, 21; *"Now when He was asked by the Pharisees when the Kingdom of God would come, He answered them and said, 'The Kingdom of God does not come with observation; nor will they say, See here! Or See there! For indeed, the kingdom of God is within you."*

This passage highlights two significant things. First, and most obvious, is that this Kingdom is not observable in the way other kingdoms are. It is 'seen' in an entirely different sense. The second thing is implied in the phrase, *'See here! Or See there!'* There will always be attempts by individuals or groups to advertise the Kingdom of God as something observable, (that is, visible to the eye) in clear contradiction of Jesus' words. Perhaps prophetically, Jesus anticipated a persistent misapprehension that would continue for twenty centuries or more.

Again, *"The Kingdom of God is within you (or among you.)"* To be more definitive, let's say it this way; **the Kingdom of God is wherever the rule of God is acknowledged in people's hearts, and among those people who mutually acknowledge it.** The Christian priority, according to Jesus, is to desire and embrace the rule and character of God for our lives. As people do that, they comprise for Him what is called the church. *"I will build My church . . ."* (Matt. 16:18) Jesus builds the church, a grand tapestry of godly relationships, past and present (Heb. 12:1), and our enemy's best efforts will not impede its continual prosperity. These are foundational truths.

As Christianity became institutionalized in the second and third centuries, the term 'church' became more and more synonymous with something visible. As the generations passed, the institution became increasingly complex, and the more resources of time, energy, and money it required to sustain its prominent role in the lives of the faithful. Soon church, for the average believer, meant a building, a clergy, a liturgy, a series of rules and prohibitions overseen by a clerical hierarchy, and varying forms of religious practice. Quite a distance from the thing Jesus said He would build. And His message of 'the Kingdom' gradually became an obscure concept; a bit of holdover religious terminology heard primarily at the reading of the parables.

Many, if not most contemporary American Christians have come to think of the very visible church as God's Kingdom on the earth; virtual synonyms. Of course, in many ways they correspond, like the rain and an umbrella correspond, but they are sometimes vastly different in their priorities and their potential. Unfortunately many modern saints never learn the dynamic relationship of the one to the other, and consequently their lives are often mere caricatures of what God intended for His people.

The organized church is truthful, purposeful, and dynamic in direct proportion to how faithfully the individuals within the church are responsive to the Kingdom. The churches in America have, for the most part, trained their members to be sustained by the functions of the organized church rather than teaching them to live by the resources of the kingdom. This is usually done unwittingly, but the evidence that this is the case is compelling.

The visible church generally consists of the facilities, the service schedule, the peer/study/support groups, the activities calendar, the volunteer programs, the outreaches, the stewardship program, the liturgy, and the clergy and his/her staff. The corporate worship experience itself is often configured in technologically assisted, easily digested sound-bytes so everyone finds it informative and stimulating. Gone are the discomforts of lengthy singing, sermons, or (God forbid) silence. And, as Eugene Peterson lamented in his devotional on **The Message**, *"the pastor has become the quality control engineer in this operation, ensuring sterling production and Christian productivity."*

In American Christianity new believers are often led in the 'sinner's prayer', or to recite a confessional of some kind, given a Bible or some literature, enrolled in the 'new converts' class, and are encouraged to study and pray. *Good things.* However, in practice, most of them are soon acclimated to the service schedule, plus a stream of activities, fellowships, projects, community service, and an ever widening circle of 'Christian' entertainment, thus finding their time, energies, and resources being tapped for the church's agenda. Consequently, many professing Christians develop what one writer called a "boarding school mentality;" that is, the church keeps them so occupied they don't realize they're actually living *a life without their Father!*

In contrast, kingdom priorities focus new saints on developing an inner awareness of, and relationship with God, the disciplines that facilitate living in the Spirit (Gal. 5:16), and the enrichment and revelation found in celebratory praise and worship with the believers. Kingdom participation is characterized by the leadership and gifts of the Spirit, nurturing a mentality of faith, private devotion (praise, prayer, and meditation), the scriptures, building godly relationships, ministry (i.e. service) to the family and the saints, remembering the poor, and keeping one's self uncontaminated from the world. (James 1:27)

Doubtless many churches advocate these things in one form or another in their founding documents or charter, but over time many of them are neglected as churches do what is necessary to sustain a population which is often self-interested, and accustomed to ease and amusement. This certainly compromises their gospel witness, and the wellbeing of the saints. **When churches fail to *function* consistent with their stated beliefs and priorities they set up huge growth barriers to the people who listen to them.**

What are We Building?

In the introduction I referenced the Apostle Paul's caution that everyone pay careful attention to how he builds on the foundation of Jesus Christ. (1 Cor. 3:10-12) It is quite possible to build impressive religious systems with little or no kingdom substance, and which leave the innocent, uninformed saints anemic and vulnerable. Paul told the early Christians that they were "God's building," that they were "God's garden." (1 Cor. 3:9) Clearly the New Testament sets out a gospel which prioritizes the cultivating of *people*.

So then, if the saints themselves, and their functional wellbeing is a gospel priority (Eph. 4:11, 12), then we must regard everything erected to support that effort as simply 'scaffolding.' By definition scaffolding is 'a temporary or movable platform for workers.' It is something useful and practical, but definitely temporary. Scaffolding doesn't get much aesthetic attention, is usually no more solid than necessary, and is intended to be short-term, torn down, moved, and thrown together again wherever needed to complete the building process. (Eph. 2:20-22) So then, we maintain that religious structures are just scaffolding; *people are what God is building.* (1 Cor. 3:9) After reading Paul for over 60 years now, I don't get much 'tongue in cheek' from him. I think he meant precisely that; *build the people.*

What is conspicuous about American Christianity is that much, and in many cases *most* of the time, energy, money, and creativity available to the church is poured into the *scaffolding*, while the people of God are assured that it is indeed God's will for them to help finance and facilitate the effort. Thus the church, by its facilities, amenities, and programs, and the people by association, are validated in the community. And all this may take place quite apart from any real kingdom activity.

Jeanie and I visited a church in a Midwestern city several years ago, and our visit corresponded with a special presentation by a 'stewardship organization,' outlining to the congregation of about four hundred their need to move from their present location (a beautiful church facility in a nice residential part of town) to a growth area of the city in order to 'secure your future.' We understood the logic of the move from a business / demographic point of view; that's how church leaders think in modern America. But the absence of any mention of God having a hand in their future, or of the thousands of people all around their present location who needed ministry was hard to comprehend in an actual Christian gathering.

The individuals involved in this rather common practice are probably well intentioned. But regardless of what is 'accepted' in church business, it is the responsibility of Christian leaders, authorities, and indeed the saints in every generation to judge whether or not the priorities and activities of the church are generated from, and informed by, everyone's vital interaction with the Kingdom of God. Sadly, the aforementioned incident is a good example of a church displaying little practical kingdom orientation. The obvious priority was to position themselves among a more affluent, more educated population; folks who will appreciate and support up-scale facilities and amenities.

The visible church, and its accompanying structures and functions, is usually begun with good intentions and for an honorable purpose. Indeed, without it some people would not be converted. But its greatest value is realized by how effectively it helps to equip and complete the Building (God's people, Coll. 2:9-10), and how it directs worship and glory to the Architect. It is a gross misunderstanding of its purpose to make it the permanent thing. *That would be like setting aside the product and bending one's efforts toward the adornment and preservation of the packaging!* Of course most churches deny doing this, but the evidence is compelling. In general, America has an obviously flourishing ecclesiastical infrastructure serving a rather anemic, self-absorbed population.

In what direction are we moving?

I ask people to grasp this principle as a clarifying agent for our thoughts and ultimately our priorities: **God is always moving us from the complex toward the simple; from bondage toward freedom.**

Right away, we're confronted by the obvious fact that institutions, religious or otherwise, are moving in precisely the opposite direction. That is, institutions / organizations invariably move from simplicity toward complexity, from freedom toward bondage. More people, more departments, more systems, more rules, less freedom, less understanding, less tolerance, less flexibility, less sensitivity, etc. That being the case, one's relationship with institutional Christianity must necessarily be careful, well informed, and light handed.

Ancient Judaism was very complex and stern. The law provided Israel with a 'constitution for life,' touching every facet of human experience; spiritual, relational, political, health and hygiene, agriculture, animal husbandry, etc. There were no exceptions, very little wiggle room in interpretation, and dire penalties for transgression. And twenty centuries of 'interpretation,' until the time of Christ, added volumes to the literature of the holy people (i.e., the Talmud), minutely detailing how life should be lived in 'righteousness' before God.

No wonder it was difficult for the Jews to accept the gospel; it was far too simple. *"Believe on the name of the Lord Jesus Christ and you shall be saved"* had to sound absurd to them. It didn't require enough, wasn't detailed enough, and offered far too much freedom. Surely there was more to it! . . . . and much like Judaism, the Christian churches through the centuries since Christ have added their own volumes of doctrines and details, which brings us to the present.

The point is, God moved men away from the complexity of ceremonial Judaism to the *"simplicity that is in Christ."* (2 Cor. 11:3) We no longer apprehend and approach God through the maze of temple, and priesthood, and sacrifice, but we now are able to clearly see Him, as J.B. Phillips put it, "through a Christ-shaped window." From complexity to simplicity.

Of course we discover in Christianity that its institutions quite easily parallel the complexity of Judaism with a vast array of 'temples, priests, ceremonies, and sacrifices' of another sort which tends, almost invariably, toward rigidity and eventual religious bondage. Again, we'll say it is mostly unintentional, but denominational, doctrinally driven, sectarian Christianity can quite easily impede the great freedoms of life-in-Christ. Full participation often results in a self-imposed quarantine from any substantive spiritual liberty by submitting to the church's hierarchies, doctrinal imperatives, cultural directives and agendas, programmed activities, and rules (written and unwritten) about almost everything.

Throughout history good men or women have tried to organize and systematize their own understanding and experience of God, hoping to encourage others to follow. We must value those efforts. However, God does not empower institutions; *He empowers people*. Over time most of these organizations become increasingly complex, sectarian, and eventually fail to give priority to the one thing God *did* 'set up,' the Kingdom, which is *in us*, and operating *among us*. (Daniel 2:44; Luke 17:21).

As others have wisely said before me, we must never allow 'Christianity' to crowd out Jesus Christ. So, it is incumbent on every believer to pursue an understanding of the nature and function of His kingdom, and become an engaged participant in it. We will also better serve the Lord and others by appreciating how the visible church may play a part in the widening influence of that kingdom. The churches have a significant role if and when their primary enterprise, not in word but in *practice*, is enlisting and spiritually equipping the ones for whom Christ died. For any religious endeavor to be considered truly Christian, it is most certainly those ends which justify the means.

5

LAST MINUTE INSTRUCTIONS

When a person who is very influential in our lives is preparing to leave us for an extended period, and he or she repeats something several times during our final meeting, most of us are going to give special attention to that matter. Well, the last time Jesus gathered with His men He did precisely that. Doubtless, every Christian will want to carefully and prayerfully heed those words. But first, a question.

Who has been made responsible for administering God's church, that is, the people of God? Does the administration (or government) of the church necessarily flow through the religious structures men have built, or is there another governing agent for His creative and redemptive activity among the saints? As we shall see, how each individual resolves that question will be significant in determining how he or she experiences life-in-Christ.

John's gospel is always very valuable, not so much for a detailed chronology of Jesus activities and teachings, but rather for John's personal insights into significant events. John 13-17 gives us an amazingly detailed summary of Jesus' final directives and encouragement to His men just prior to his arrest later in the evening. Beginning by washing His disciple's feet, Jesus taught them about true greatness, about His peace, about 'abiding' in Him. He gave the great command to 'love one another,' He spoke about persecution, and about how to engage the Father after His departure. And finally, He prayed for them.

What is remarkable about this passage is that interspersed with these important truths John recalled five distinct occasions when Jesus promised the advent of the Holy Spirit, and explained how vital the Spirit would be to their understanding and experience of the things He was sharing with them. He told them there were many things they would need to remember in the future but the Holy Spirit would bring His words back to them. In fact, He said it was to their advantage for Him to go back to the Father because the Spirit would bring a universal revelation of 'sin, righteousness, and judgment.' *"I have many things to say to you, but you cannot bear them now,"* He said. *"However, when the Spirit of truth has come, He will guide you into all truth . . ."*

Clearly, Jesus' greatest emphasis in His last minute instructions was the importance of receiving and continually responding to 'The Helper,' the Holy Spirit, who would clarify, amplify, and further detail His words to them throughout their lifetime. Everything He pledged to them that night would be made possible by the Spirit working through them. *"He dwells with you and will be in you,"* He promised them. The Spirit would speak of Jesus, glorify Jesus, and convey to their spirit only those things He hears, for He will never be speaking on His own authority. *"And,"* Jesus said, *"He will show you things to come."* His final prayer shows the universal scope of His word about the Spirit; *"I do not pray for these alone, but also for those who will believe in Me through their word; that they all may be one . . ."* (John 17:20, 21)

The heartache and confusion of the next few days were a great crisis in the Apostle's lives. Betrayed, forsaken by His own, Jesus was arrested, tried, abused and tortured by the Romans, and finally crucified to satiate the hatred of the Jewish religious establishment. Jesus words of promise from that night must have seemed hollow and distant to the Apostles . . . . except His personal word to Peter; *"Will you lay down your life for My sake? Most assuredly I say to you, the rooster shall not crow till you have denied me three times!"*

The resurrection stunned everyone. It took days, weeks, for Jesus followers to absorb this new reality. It was not easy. So *"He also presented Himself alive after his suffering by many infallible proofs, being seen by them during forty days and speaking of the things pertaining to the kingdom of God."* Remarkable days, by any account. But in His final moments with them, once again *"He commanded them not to depart from Jerusalem, but to wait for the Promise of the Father . . . . You shall be baptized with the Holy Spirit not many days from now."*

As Jesus' startling ascension into heaven was beginning to unfold on the Mount of Olives, He left His beloved with a parting pledge, *"You shall receive power when the Holy Spirit is come upon you, and you shall be witnesses to Me in Jerusalem, and in all Judea and Samaria, and to the end of the earth."* Well, they believed His word, and for more than a week they were gathered *"with one accord in prayer and supplication"* in an upstairs hall, waiting . . . . *"till suddenly there came a sound from heaven."* (Acts 1:8, 14; 2:2)

The advent of the Holy Spirit is, next to the resurrection, the most significant and defining event in the New Testament. The early disciples were presented with a gospel that could be proclaimed not only "in word but in power." (1 Cor. 4:20) Also, they were introduced to the Spirit of God as an indwelling presence, granting them access to understanding, insight, and empowerment through faith in Jesus Christ and by acting in His name.

Everything Jesus had promised the Apostles the night of His passion now became a dynamic reality for them, and for the other believers present at Pentecost. And not only that, Peter declared to the assembled crowd that what they were seeing and hearing was for everyone! *"Repent, and let every one of you be baptized in the name of Jesus Christ for the remission of sins, and you shall receive the gift of the Holy Spirit. For the promise is to you and to your children, and to all who are afar off, as many as the Lord our God will call."* (Acts 2: 38, 39)

There is no evidence *from scripture* that God, the Holy Spirit ever deviated from the pattern at Pentecost. Whenever individuals or groups, Jews or Gentiles, believed the gospel and put their trust in Jesus' death and resurrection for the forgiveness of sins, they received, either by a sovereign work of God or by the laying on of hands, the gift of the Holy Spirit. Energized by the indwelling presence of Jesus, they became a bold prophetic company.

The Book of Acts chronicles this with great simplicity and clarity. Following a rigorous questioning and threats by the Jewish Sanhedrin about the healing of the lame man (Acts 3:1-8), the Apostles rejoined the other believers for a time of prayer for courage and boldness. *"And when they had prayed, the place where they were assembled together was shaken, and they were all filled with the Holy Spirit."* (Acts 4:23-31)

The Apostle Philip had a fruitful ministry in Samaria, with many turning to the Lord. When the Apostles at Jerusalem heard this good news they sent Peter and John. The two Apostles immediately *"prayed for them that they might receive the Holy Spirit. For as yet He had fallen upon none of them. They had only been baptized in the name of the Lord Jesus. Then they laid hands on them, and they received the Holy Spirit."* (Acts 8:5-17) On this occasion the impact of the Spirit on the believers was so evident and profound that Simon, a sorcerer, offered money to the Apostles for such power.

The conversion of Saul of Tarsus is another example. After being struck down from his horse by the Lord on his way to Damascus, He was blinded and was three days in that condition.

Finally the Spirit spoke to a believer named Ananias about Saul, and instructed him to lay hands on him *"that you might receive your sight and be filled with the Holy Spirit."* (Acts 9:1-17)

The account of Peter's vision in which God commanded him to 'call no man unclean,' and the ensuing plea from the Centurion Cornelius for him to come to Caesarea and preach to his gentile household is a marvelous narrative! The result was, *"as Peter was still speaking these words (about Jesus Christ), the Holy Spirit fell upon all those who heard the word. And those of the circumcision who believed were astonished, as many as came with Peter, because the gift of the Holy Spirit had been poured out on the gentiles also. For they heard them speak with tongues and magnify God."* (Acts 10:44-46)

As Peter rehearsed the story of Cornelius' conversion to the skeptical leaders at Jerusalem, some tried to censure him for having any commerce with non-Jews. Peter finished his defense by saying, *"As I began to speak, the Holy Spirit fell upon them, **as upon us at the beginning.** Then I remembered the word of the Lord, how He said, 'John indeed baptized with water, but you shall be baptized with the Holy Spirit.' If therefore God gave them the same gift as He gave us when we believed on the Lord Jesus Christ, who was I that I could withstand God?"* (Acts 11:1-17)

Occasionally the early church would encounter people who had heard John the Baptist or some of his disciples, and had submitted to the 'baptism of repentance' that John preached. Paul found about a dozen such folks at Ephesus. After preaching Jesus to them *"they were baptized in the name of the Lord Jesus. And when Paul had laid hands of them, the Holy Spirit came upon them, and they spoke with tongues and prophesied."* (Acts 19:1-7) As one continues throughout the Acts, the instruction and power of the Holy Spirit is clearly evident in the decisions, movements, and ministry of the Apostles and prophets. Although not every instance of individuals coming to the Lord is described by Luke in such detail, it's clear from the previous examples that the early church considered the infilling of the Spirit an essential part of conversion and discipleship.

Beyond the Apostles and into the second century, the record reflects this continuing work of the Spirit. Catholic authors McDonnell and Montague, in their marvelous pamphlet, **Fanning the Flame**, put it this way:

> How did the early post-biblical church appropriate this biblical teaching? Baptism in the Holy Spirit was a synonym for Christian initiation in Justin Martyr, Origen, Didymus the Blind, Cyril of Jerusalem, Tertullian, Hilary of Poitiers, John Chrysostom, John of Apamea, Severus of Antioch, and Joseph Hazzaya. Their testimony demonstrates that the infilling of the Holy Spirit is not a matter of private piety, but of the official liturgy, and of the church's public life. . . . we believe that this gift of the baptism in the Holy Spirit belongs to the Christian inheritance of all those sacramentally initiated into the church. (pps. 15, 16, 10; Fanning the Flame, 1991; Order of St. Benedict)

Manifestly, from the words of Jesus, and from the example and instruction of the early church leaders, the Holy Spirit had become the administrator of His kingdom. That administration would originate in the sanctuary of every believer's heart, quietly energizing, encouraging, directing, and cautioning him as he moves through the complicated maze of human existence. Where once Moses, and prophets, judges, priests, and finally Jesus Himself had directed God's people, now the Spirit of

Jesus Christ (Rom. 8:9) would faithfully represent the interests of God in their lives.

This was radically new ground, especially for the Jewish believers, who were conditioned by centuries of Tabernacle / Temple practice to approach God in a prescribed way. But the Apostles understood that in Jesus Christ *God had come to them*, and the leadership of the Spirit was simply the continuation of that very personal relationship with their Lord they had experienced for three years, walking with Him in the flesh.

"This is what was spoken by the prophet Joel," Peter shouted to the incredulous throng at Pentecost. *"And it shall come to pass in the last days, says God, that I will pour out of My Spirit on all flesh . . . . . and it shall come to pass that whoever calls on the name of the Lord shall be saved."* (Acts 2: 16, 17, 21) The Apostles knew to expect something revolutionary, for Jesus had made no indication that they were to form an 'up-dated' version of Judaism. No, something entirely new and transcendent was upon them.

A Principle or a Person?

In light of everything I've just rehearsed, it's important to observe that a large cross-section of the modern church gives little more than doctrinal acknowledgement to the existence of the Holy Spirit, and often even less attention to what He might be doing or saying in the moment. He is often perceived as an 'influence,' or as a sort of *spiritual enthusiasm* for Christian living, but hardly as the Holy Facilitator for everything pertaining to Jesus Christ. He is mentioned and consulted rarely, given only titular billing on the church's busy agenda.

The reason for this is difficult to analyze without passing judgement. Suffice it to say, relating to an invisible deity is challenging for all of us at times, and one need only revisit the Old

Testament account of the 'golden calf' to appreciate how quickly God's people, and their consenting leaders, can detour toward religious activity that is more to their preferences, and more acceptable to the tastes of the surrounding culture. (Exodus 32:1-6)

I believe the operative phrase for the Christian life is Romans 8:26, *"The Spirit also helps in our weaknesses."* This is a promise that should comfort and fortify every believer. But rather than embracing the Holy Spirit as the central dynamic of the Christian life, much of the church is embarrassed by the spectacle of Pentecost and has carefully constructed a doctrinal bunker to protect themselves from it.

Through much of the twentieth century, dispensationalist theology deeply and negatively impacted a large portion of the traditional churches where the Holy Spirit is concerned. *"Having a form of godliness but denying the power thereof"* (2 Tim. 3:5) sounds perilously close to describing how some groups slighted the Holy Spirit; particularly in recognizing His presence within the public functions of the church. "Those things (gifts or manifestations of the Spirit) passed away with the Apostles," many churches taught. Thankfully, that position has moderated in many groups during the past couple of decades as the Spirit has continued to impact and empower increasing millions around the world, bearing witness to His sustained fulfillment of Jesus emphatic promise.

Regrettably, some groups have become very doctrinaire about the baptism in the Spirit, insisting that believers speak, act, and even dress in a certain way to 'evidence' the reality of the Spirit's activity in their lives. But that too is a disservice to the interests of Jesus who said, *"The wind blows where it wishes, and you can hear the sound of it, but cannot tell where it comes from and where it goes. **So is everyone who is born of the Spirit.**"* (John 3:8) It is impossible to 'pin down' exactly how the Spirit will or should manifest himself through a particular believer, any more than one can predict or manipulate the wind. As we've demonstrated, the New Testament gives us some clear examples of the dynamic impact of the Spirit on the believers, but His ongoing work is not subject to any group's specifications; only to the purposes of the Father. That is, empower every Christian, in some unique and personal way, to experience, exemplify, and glorify Jesus Christ.

As Theologian Karl Barth wisely stated, "The word of God can stand for itself. It is not for sale, therefore it needs no skilled salesmen." The New Testament in its entirety graphically illustrates that Jesus' disciples had experienced something extraordinary at Pentecost, and clearly their objective was to share that same experience of transformation and power with everyone who would receive it. Again, the "promise of the Father" (Acts 1:4) is both *scriptural* and potently practical.

Of course, the wisdom and guidance of godly Pastors, Evangelists, Prophets and Teachers may also be an enriching part of a believers' life, and we should eagerly avail ourselves of those ministry gifts. But the primary function of these spiritual authorities is to establish the *authority of God* in the lives of the saints, and that administration is carried out moment to moment by the Holy Spirit.

It is no small challenge for church leaders to consistently acknowledge and support the governance of the Holy Spirit in the lives of the saints. It requires a continually calibrated kingdom perspective, recognizing the potential in *every* believer. And perhaps an even greater challenge for church leaders is to also be responsive to the Spirit in the daily functions of the organization. No saint is exempt; the folks in the pulpits are as accountable to His authority as the folks in the pews. *Institutional Christianity will be kingdom significant in direct proportion to her leaders' commitment to being Spirit-led rather than church driven.*

Every redeemed man and woman is given the privilege of living as Jesus lived, replicating (however imperfectly) a life lived under the Spirit's loving administration. Christ's nature is revealed in them through the fruit of the Spirit (Gal. 5:22): *"Love, joy, peace, longsuffering, kindness, goodness, faithfulness, gentleness, self-control."* The ministry of Jesus is perpetuated through them in spiritual gifts (1 Cor. 12:7-10): *"But the manifestation of the Spirit is given to each one for the profit of all; for to one is given the word of wisdom through the Spirit, to another the word of knowledge through the same Spirit, to another faith by the same Spirit, to another gifts of healing through the same Spirit, to another the working of miracles, to another prophecy, to another discerning of spirits, to another different kinds of tongues, to another the interpretation of tongues. But one and the same Spirit works all these things, distributing to each one individually as He wills."*

In the same way that the nature of the Lord and His power for service are imparted to us by the Holy Spirit, the guidance necessary for living them fully also comes by the same Spirit. Like the Lord Jesus, believers may do and say what they hear from the Father. (Ref. John 6, 8, 12, 14) *"My sheep hear My voice, and I know them, and they follow Me."* (John 10:27) Lighting our way, too, should always be the scriptures, both the Old and New Testament. After all, why should we expect to receive the word we *need* if we don't value the Word we *have*?

So, in the everyday transactions of life, God's church, that is, *the saints* are invited by the Lord to enjoy the fellowship and facilitating power of the Holy Spirit as their primary engagement with Him. *A personal relationship indeed!*

6

'OUR DAILY BREAD'

Only one enduring image is passed on by our Lord;
a powerful visual He clearly staged the last time
He gathered with His disciples before His passion.

Jesus introduced His ministry with the declaration, *'The kingdom
of God has come near,'* and I want to highlight yet another witness to
that remarkable reality, and our very personal involvement in it.
Earlier I paid tribute to my parents, Bob and Lois, and to their
hospitality; *"Hearts came open around their table."* That was quite purposeful, because the very spirit of **You are the Plan** calls for some
kind of symbolic representation to help us understand it, and for a
way to celebrate it with simplicity and practicality day to day.

Well, the truth is, Jesus Himself has provided that symbol for
us. He puts our relationship with Him, and with one another, in
a distinct context; one which every saint can relate to and draw
insight from.

Symbols play an important role in our lives. We are surrounded by icons, art, and ads, all symbols of a sort, which remind us to
buy, or give, or behave a certain way. Christianity has always been

represented by symbols. The cross, the fish, a lamp, a sheep, the empty tomb, the Madonna, and praying hands; these are all powerful reminders to the popular consciousness of various aspects of the Christian faith.

However, the New Testament, and Jesus in particular, gave us none of these as a bona fide representation of the faith. Only one enduring image is passed on by our Lord; a powerful visual He clearly staged the last time He gathered with His beloved disciples before His passion. That image and symbol is *a table* (Luke 22:14-20; 1 Cor. 11:23-34).

Some would argue that the cross should have that distinction, and that's understandable. *"God forbid that I should glory except in the cross of our Lord Jesus Christ, by whom the world is crucified to me, and I to the world."* (Galatians 6:14) Without question the redemptive center of Christianity is the cross and the shedding of innocent blood for our sins. It frames for all men for all time the grace and love of God toward them. We must never be separated from that great truth. But it is precisely because we need to remember the cross that *the table* then becomes so significant for the faith community, generation to generation.

Virtually every Christian group acknowledges that the very ordinary acts of eating and drinking have become a primary means by which we acknowledge His broken body and shed blood, and through their efficacy we collectively participate in the New Covenant. The sacrament of the "Lord's Supper" has, for twenty centuries, been the simple celebratory rite binding the universal Body of Christ together. This covenantal symbol of Christianity, a table, reinforces for us our identification with Christ both in the Spirit and in our shared humanity, and suggests some very important and precious things for saints embracing **You are the Plan.**

YOU ARE THE PLAN 53

Perhaps the most obvious is that there is a table in almost every dwelling, even the most humble. This fact brings the sacramental realities much closer to us, with the startling implication that our *everyday eating and drinking may actually be a powerful part of our Communion with God.* The table is the gathering place of a household, reminding us that a primary unit of redemption is the family, not simply the individual (Ex. 12; "a lamb for a family"; Acts 11:14). A great many spiritual transactions may take place at the table where folks acknowledge the Holy Presence in their 'daily bread.'

The table is a place of acceptance, where God's provision is shared with all. The family, their guests, even the stranger, are united by the common need for food and human fraternity. For those moments of refreshment our differences and blemishes are diminished. When King David took the lame Mephibosheth into his care for Jonathan's sake (2 Samuel 9:13), we were given a clear picture of this. *His feet under the King's table, his infirmity became of no significance!*

It is across a table that we meet each other face to face, not in rows, in a crowd, or standing in the same line. We are 'eye to eye,' and it is there that the issues of life are often resolved by getting things 'on the table.' Many of the ancient peoples would not share a meal with contention or distrust in the air. It dishonored the table.

For the present time, this symbol helps to focus us on the heart of God for His people. *"A new commandment I give you . . . that you love one another."* The table reminds us that this love is not so much spiritual as it is practical, a love lived out morning, noon, and night, demonstrated through the most basic transactions of life.

Countless times over the years Jeanie and I have experienced the grace of God around our table. Sometimes with friends, church folks, ministry associates, or a half dozen college students our boys brought home with them for the holidays. When believers gather around a table, *kingdom stuff happens.* Many of the great ideas and images from the Bible occurred during or after a meal.

The table has a definite eschatological dimension as well. *"Behold, I stand at the door and knock. If anyone hears My voice and opens the door I will come in and eat with him and he with Me."* This is the redemptive invitation of Revelation 3:20. It is a picture of fellowship with the Lord in the most human sense. And this theme carries forward to the consummation when the Bridegroom finally receives His Bride at the 'invitation only' Marriage Supper of the Lamb (Rev. 19:9).

Is it possible that every meal in a believing household can be an occasion to 'examine' ourselves, and properly discern the Lord's Body? (1 Cor. 11:28, 29) An opportunity to bring 'body and blood' to bear on the immediate needs and problems? Most certainly. However, that does not depreciate in any way the formal celebration of the Lord's Supper. There is a distinct blessing and beauty associated with the 'enactment' of the communion in the corporate church setting. But at the same time, the very essence of the table's symbolism cries out for the wider application of its truth.

It has been suggested that whenever Christian practice is distanced from the table and its relational intimacy, 'the faith' begins to lose part of its distinct character. A significant element of our humanity from time immemorial has been our involvement with cooking and eating food. As our culture has begun to cook less and gather at our common table with less frequency it has surrendered an important part of its soul. Perhaps the saints should help balance the prevalent *corporate* emphasis of Christianity by returning to hospitality and a more personal engagement with others.

Just as regeneration has invited every person to genuinely participate in the priestly office (1 Peter 2:5, 9; Rev. 1:6), *the Living God among His people brings the merits of Jesus' atoning work across the threshold of everyone's house.* Perhaps at the table, more than anywhere else, we're aware that the kingdom has 'come near,' and we have become glad participants in it. As we gather around it with family and friends, **You are the Plan** reminds us not only to be thankful for our 'daily bread,' but to also celebrate the environment of understanding, reconciliation, and healing God has provided around us, and in us. Let's expect 'hearts to come open' around *our* table! In both reality and in symbol, the kingdom is in the house!

7

CHURCH – A LIVING THING

"The leading cause of business failure is business success"

—a banker

Jesus Christ was a success because He never deviated from the one thing He was incarnated to do; follow His Father's leading to the cross. It was the *devil* who offered Him the things that would have given Him status; made Him a social and religious celebrity. (Matt. 4:1-11) The American church often confuses "faithful" with "successful;" in this conversation they are terms from competing kingdoms.

The 1980's was an interesting decade in American Christianity with the emergence of many mega-churches throughout the country. Leadership clinics proliferated, particularly among the ever-competitive evangelicals, teaching ministers, young and old, how to build larger congregations, and crunching the scriptures to imply that several gentile churches in the New Testament enjoyed membership in the tens of thousands. Numbers, dollars, and dimensions spelled spiritual success, or the 'blessing of God.'

The rationale for this movement was that bigger churches are naturally better than smaller ones because greater numbers represent more souls. Bigger means more substantial, offering more things to more people. The larger the assembly the more impact it will have on the community, and even on the world. While this sounds quite reasonable, there is scant evidence that 'bigger is better' actually translates to a more positive *spiritual* impact on individual believers. "Success is a lousy teacher," Bill Gates warned. "It seduces smart people into thinking they can't lose." Unfortunately, in the case of many churches, the *loss* is experienced by the 'rank and file' saints while the organizations continue to tabulate their perceived successes.

Today many churches, and their corresponding organizations, continue to cherish the American socio-economic ideal of unlimited growth. At present, there are dozens of churches in this country who claim a membership of twenty thousand or more. I choose to argue, on the other hand, that the *dimensions* of a particular ministry activity may not be truly reflective of its actual spiritual impact. (1 Samuel 14:6) We're looking for God's point of view.

Permit, if you will, a small personal example. In the early 1980's Jeanie and I were asking the Lord for clarity about future ministry efforts, and during that time we held some Bible studies in a few homes. A couple of them really 'took off,' in terms of attendance, but curiously, within a few weeks they had run their course. We were disappointed and confused by that. Some really good things had happened in each meeting, and we assumed it would be more enduring. The experience left us with unsettling questions.

However, over the years of pastoring Fayetteville Christian Fellowship, we gained some perspective. Every year or two someone would approach me with words like these; "Pastor, you probably don't remember this but back in the early 80's I visited a home meeting you were ministering in and there the Lord changed my life." The lesson for us was simple: not everything with kingdom significance is *big* or *permanent*.

In fact, every organism, or *living thing*, has an optimum size, and if it grows bigger than that it will experience health problems and eventually serious impairment. Humans or hamsters, goats or giraffes, it's the same. Bones won't support it, heart can't nourish it, etc. Similarly, a fellowship of believers is a living entity and it must expect that, depending on its leaders, its location, the composition of its population, and its particular spiritual assignment for that place and time, its optimum size may be quite different from another meeting across town. *Every Christian gathering is a unique species.*

As Churches grow the people they serve are distanced further and further from the core nutrients that gave birth and life to the work. With few exceptions, the saints will have less contact with their mentors, who are themselves occupied by increasing demands. Parishioners will now be served by intermediaries who may not be as trusted or effective as the leader. Through no one's fault, the organization slowly becomes something different, with changing faces, functions, and priorities, and therefore it doesn't impact people in the same way.

In many cases, the American church sacrifices the personal voice and touch of a pastor or teacher on the altar of numerical growth. Jesus chose just twelve individuals to be the primary depository for His gospel. Although there is no scriptural or practical mandate to get large numbers of believers together under one roof, it is often promoted in our culture in order to validate someone's success or gifts. But remember, Pentecost changed the world by empowering a mere 120 souls. (Acts 1:15) I'd say that was an 'optimum sized' congregation.

I have known of several churches who aspired to greater numbers, and having built 'a bigger barn' (Luke 12:18), they found that the environment was not the same, not what they had hoped for. How often people fail to appreciate God's blessing on a particular time and place, and callously trample that precious environment in an effort to expand or export it!

Isn't our perspective better served by viewing the church (which is people) *organically* rather than organizationally? That is, we should approach the church is a *living community*, comprised of a very diverse population of redeemed human beings whose lives, in almost every area, undergo significant changes over time. A church population, small or large, cannot be expected to remain static, fixed, in its perspective, its presentation, its needs, or its abilities for an extended period. Apart from significant changes in individuals, there will be an ebb and flow of attendance, changes in the surrounding socio/economic context, and generational fluctuations which cannot be predicted or controlled. You might say it begins to *age*.

As much as church leaders would like to think their particular paradigm for 'church' is timeless, it is not. Living things have a birth, a maturation process, a period of productivity in accord with its species, an aging period and an end. This is also true of many ministries. For example, some ministries spring from a revival or a revelation of some kind and consequently experience significant growth and spiritual fruitfulness. Praise God! But usually the dynamic or circumstances that gave birth to that particular movement dissipates for whatever reason, and those saints must then find a balanced, biblically informed perspective about what they represent and how they should function going forward.

Over time, many of those ministries 'run their course;' that is, the particular spiritual experience, revelation, or individual(s) that launched that effort is somehow no longer impacting the work as before. *It is not a tragedy to recognize when that assignment, and the corresponding movement of the Spirit, has been completed!* Nevertheless, the ministry often continues, sustained by its well-honed message, its traditions, its endowment, talented leaders, and committed populations. We might say many of them are living on 'life support,' maintaining their existence by largely artificial means. The truth is, *nothing* is permanent in the realm of human beings. Everything has a life cycle, and that is as natural and predictable as the sunrise tomorrow.

Christian people, understanding this, should be comfortable seeing the Body of Christ as a continually changing organism, requiring the saints and their leaders to listen to the Spirit for insight about size, and shape, and structure, and how to continue telling the Story. We all learn fairly soon that the Christian life is all about *change*! The gospel of Jesus Christ remains the same, but often the Holy Spirit must introduce a fresh wind of revelation *outside* the existing forms and structures so that another generation can be initiated into Christ in an environment of openness and liberty. That is not an indictment of the older movement; God values their day and time just as He will value this new one! It is an ongoing challenge for every Christian endeavor to present the message in both a language and setting that succeeding generations can understand and function in with freedom. (2 Cor. 3:17) In order to do that, it is vastly more important to be enlightened by the Holy Spirit than to have state-of-the-art church accessories!

This doesn't mean the saints should never create a structured ministry or build a building. These can be useful tools in ways we've referenced before. What is vital to every servant of God, however, is the preservation of a kingdom perspective, which enables them to value these tools, but also gives them the ability to move past them or modify them when, for whatever reason, they are no longer helping to produce a robust spiritual life in the saints. The tools are not holy; *people are!* It's not a complicated viewpoint; it's just very difficult to implement because people cling to things they've created, insisting that they endure because of the people's investment in them.

In my experience, it's a lot like writing. In the course of a project one might compose a paragraph or section that is very creative, or witty, or even controversial, but as the editing process begins you find there is really no appropriate place for those thoughts. They came as an inspiration, perhaps, but they don't really add to this particular bit of work. Deleting them is hard! *'That's some good stuff,'* you think to yourself, and it really tests your commitment to the project to acknowledge those particular thoughts are out of place in it. How much *more* difficult it is to part with generations-long ideas, traditions, or locations. 'Forsaking all' can occur more than once in our journey with the Lord, and it can sorely test our commitment to *His* interests rather than our own.

The point is, when we choose to see 'church' as an organic entity, with an almost infinite variety of shapes and expressions, then we become free to do the thing God puts in *our* heart without concern for how it conforms to some religious template. Whether it is large or small, enduring or temporary, unique or oft-repeated; those issues are insignificant to the larger question, *"Is this effort bringing the grace and power of Jesus Christ to bear on people's lives; teaching and encouraging them, fellowshipping or worshipping with them, feeding and clothing them, or freeing them to follow His call?"*

We don't have to do it big, or sustain it over a long time for our service to be kingdom strategic and very meaningful to our Father. The important thing is our heart-felt response to His gentle leading. Someone said, "Anything worth doing is worth doing well." Certainly we should lend our best efforts to what we do for others, and for the kingdom. But I think it can be better stated for the benefit of all; "Anything worth doing, is *worth doing*, regardless of how well you do it." *Willingness* and *obedience*, not performance and productivity, are the watchwords of this kingdom.

8

A CRITICAL ADJUSTMENT

I'm urging the saints to create 'the world according to Jesus' for themselves.

American Christianity is at a significant juncture in its history, as more of our society is finding organized religion less relevant to their daily existence. This decline has been most significant among traditional Protestant groups and Catholicism, but Evangelical churches have also experienced a reduction in attendance. Increasing numbers of professing Christians no longer identify with a particular group. (Pew Research poll, 2015) The gospel message is still powerful but much of the American delivery system for it, as vast as it appears, is often straying or struggling. Should we attempt to reform our institutions, hundreds of them, or should some of them be slowly dismantled or replaced? Neither of these options are really practical, and most importantly, they overlook God's resource of choice for getting things done; *the saints!* (Ezekiel 22:30)

God's people are being challenged to take 'ownership' of 'the faith which was once for all delivered to the saints.' (Jude 3)

In fact, Jude wrote his little note to urge the people of God to 'earnestly contend' for the purity and simplicity of the gospel. His entire letter is an expose' of men attempting to take 'the faith' hostage to religion; religion as a cover for permissiveness, rebellion, hypocrisy, greed, flattery, manipulation, and generally pervasive worldliness. (vs. 4-16)

In order for the kingdom of God to function as He intended, organically, it needs to be driven by *living things,* not systems. Jude reminds the church that the faith (i.e. the gospel) was given *'to the saints.'* It is not the property of institutions, denominations, or religious professionals to dissect and distribute as they see fit. It is *our* faith, yours and mine. To 'take ownership' means to accept part of the responsibility for the message, to set a high value on one's own experience and understanding of it, and to take seriously the trust God has placed in his people as representatives of Jesus Christ. (2 Cor. 5:17-20) We can all tell the story, and though each of us will tell it with a little different flavor, it will nonetheless be genuine; "*My* gospel," as the Apostle Paul liked to call it.

Jesus asked the disciples what the crowds were saying about Him. (Luke 9:18-20) They shared what they'd heard; *"He's John the Baptist, Elijah, or one of the old prophets risen again."* Jesus' response to their report is kingdom strategic; *"But who do **you** say that I am?"*

The gospel is God's message of love and hope for each individual; for his or her family, friends, and neighbors. In it are the building blocks for all of life. (2 Peter 1:3) *Taking ownership of the gospel causes virtually everything in our lives to become infused with Jesus.* We don't have to go anywhere, or be with anyone in particular to walk

YOU ARE THE PLAN   65

in fellowship with Him, and serve kingdom interests. Just as the Spirit has become the medium or environment in which we live and move by faith, the gospel is the vocabulary 'seasoning' our conversation with the surrounding culture. The gospel, *the faith*, is our identifying 'accent,' revealing our citizenship in the kingdom of God.

To 'own it' is to take responsibility for it *in our world*. The gospel of Jesus Christ is a sacred trust given us by the Lord Himself. This will motivate us to learn how to 'walk in the Spirit' (Gal. 5:16), be 'led of the Spirit' (Romans 8:14), and navigate our way around all the fads, fashion, trends, and personality worship that so easily distract many believers and churches.

I'm urging the saints to create 'the world according to Jesus' for themselves. Over the years I've listened to hundreds of saints complain about churches; they can never seem to find that one perfect place where everyone believes and behaves like they want them to. Well, *no* church can live up to that demand; that's an unreasonable expectation. But I understand what people want to experience in their walk with Jesus; a sense of *community*, shared faith and fellowship with some folks who also value their vision and understanding.

Well, when we take ownership of the gospel we accept the honor of being agents of the kingdom within the environment we affect. The goal is to make our world a place of peace, fellowship, and consistent praise and glory to the Lord. In short, we decide that, *'as much as depends on us'* (Romans 12:18), we're going to promote the kind of world we'd like to live, and work, and worship in. And in so doing, by God's grace we'll bump into some other like-minded folks to share that vision and journey with us.

Obviously, this will not happen simply by a decision, but it must surely *begin* there. God uses people who value His word, who can decide for themselves what the scriptures are calling for, and who will bring the resources of faith, family, and friends to bear on making that happen. It is a life-long process, to be sure, but we are the ones who reap the most benefit, while at the same time making 'the world according to Jesus' more visible for the people around us. Creating that 'world' isn't about associating with the right movement, or party, or trend. It's about a man or woman's sincere desire to *become something of God* that will affect the circle of folks around them, and enable Him to draw others into that circle as Jesus is seen and exalted.

It is generally true that when one 'owns' something he's more disposed to really value it and care for it. *Jesus wants His words in our hands, in our mouths.* Unlike some religious authorities, the saints have no professional interest in using His words to impress, control, condemn, or exploit people. The gospel has brought life to us and our loved ones, and because that is so, we are most apt to handle it lovingly, carefully, and sincerely. God knows that; that's why **You are the Plan**.

And just as significant for the future, when we take ownership of the gospel we free the churches from the unreasonable burden of trying to keep us committed, engaged, and even entertained. Many sincere souls expect the churches to cleanse and energize them week to week; a kind of spiritual dialysis for their ongoing toxicity. *The saints don't live like that.* We seize daily the power of the word and the Spirit to maintain a kingdom orientation, thereby enabling us to bring *to the church* an expectant faith that helps lift us, and the other saints, into a meaningful engagement with God.

Of course, none of us are consistently 'on top of the world' at every Christian gathering, but our expectation for relief and encouragement should be focused on the One who loves us, not on other saints. In that way, the church can more readily discharge her calling to pray for, and help *facilitate* healing without having to pose as the Healer.

God has put in store for us the power to impact, first our own broken selves, and subsequently the needy souls that surround us daily. Simple people, in union with Jesus through his Spirit, are the means to bring the message of the kingdom of heaven into everyman's world. Believe that, and own it! There's no frenzied agenda, no heavenly deadline to meet. Just be faithful and real when the opportunity comes. Remember, *"The word is near you, even in your mouth and in your heart."*

> *"How beautiful are the feet of those who preach the gospel of peace, who bring glad tidings of good things."* Isaiah, prophet and poet, *saw you coming!* (Isaiah 52:7)

9

VALUING THE ENVIRONMENT

*"The main thing about Christianity is not the work we do, but the relationship (with God) we maintain, **and the atmosphere produced by that relationship.** That is all God asks us to look after, and it is the one thing that is being constantly assailed."*

—Oswald Chambers.

Some of this section will be relatively subjective, drawing on experiences that are particularly valuable to Jeanie and me, but which some readers may not share with us. Nonetheless, I hope you will consider its premise and apply it as both heart and mind commends.

I've always been a sports fan. It's exciting to enter a stadium or arena and sense the anticipation as the stands begin to fill. It's an atmosphere that fans relish and elaborately prepare for. There's no problem getting people focused or engaged! Not every environment is that stimulating, of course, but responding appropriately to varying environments is vital in every facet of our existence.

For example, if it's 20 degrees outside, you're going to want to dress warmly. If you're meeting your girlfriend's parents for the first time, you'll probably want to look nice and behave yourself. If you've been asked to speak to a group of 6th graders, you'll doubtless avoid big words and talking for very long. It's all part of knowing what is appropriate for a particular time, place, or situation.

Christian people should be aware of not only the external demands of a certain setting, but also develop a sensitivity to the present spiritual climate as well, whether in our homes, at work, in social contexts, or in the gathering of saints. When Paul reasoned with the Greek intellectuals in Athens he described God as the very medium of human existence; *"In Him we live, and move, and have our being."* (Acts 17:28) David reflected on the immediacy of God's presence in Psalm 139; *"Where can I go from Your Spirit? Or where can I flee from Your presence? If I ascend into heaven, You are there; if I make my bed in hell, behold, You are there."* (vs.7, 8) Holy men have always recognized that God's person fills the universe He has created.

However, as we've discussed before, God is now both present and available for His saints in a unique and powerful way in the person of the Holy Spirit. I want to rehearse the very potent pledge Jesus made to His disciples; *"Where two or three are gathered in My name, there I will be among them."* (Matt. 18:20)

Let me restate that promise as I understand it. ***Every time Christian people congregate, particularly for the purposes of the kingdom, the Spirit of God will impact that gathering with His presence.*** This is true whether the venue is an arena or a living room, whether it was planned or spontaneous, involving a crowd or a handful. For our purpose here, we'll be speaking primarily about the purposeful assembly of believers, the event we usually call 'church.'

How the Christian gathering is perceived and conducted is germane to our subject because of the obvious tension in American Christianity between organization and environment. In most cases, this tension leads to the neglect or compromise of the environment, or atmosphere; the very thing Oswald Chambers cautioned us to protect.

For the purpose of discussion, we're going to say these terms represent two primary models for corporate church function; **organizational** and **environmental**. How church leaders choose between the two, assuming they actually have a choice, depends largely on their perception of reality. Without question, one of these models makes things more predictable, and therefore it is much more prevalent than the other.

If God has simply prescribed for us a religious regimen to follow, which might include our affiliation, attendance at public worship, a form, ritual, or liturgy for guidance, support for the programs, etc., then the organizational model is most appropriate. On the other hand, if God *actually involves Himself* in the corporate worship experience in more than simply a sacramental way . . . . in other words, if fire might occasionally 'fall on the altar,' so to speak, then a sensitivity to the environment is of greater importance. (1 Kings 18:36-39)

To advocate for the environmental model doesn't imply that organization and agenda are not valuable. They are indeed. What is at issue is priority. Organization allows us to proceed in an orderly way. Most church people appreciate knowing their leaders have given forethought to the 'menu;' nevertheless, something served *fresh* or *special* is always an energizer. The environmental model makes room for revelation, insight, inspiration, and even the miraculous within the planned agenda. In other words, God is invited to participate as a Person.

Organization, as we're describing it, usually also implies a schedule and prescribed participants. Some groups call this the 'order of service,' or the program, or the liturgy. In most sectors of American Christianity one of these is followed, usually very strictly. However, *there is a distinct atmosphere produced by the presence of God when true believers gather.* Whether the congregants recognize it or not, that atmosphere is very active, organic, and full of potential. God among His people is a formula for something enriching and quite possibly unexpected. It is easy to see that might create some tension for an organization, and consequently most organizations clarify their intent to follow the preplanned format. They maintain that authority. Unfortunately the result is often this: the people of God and/or the Spirit of God may have little to do with what transpires in the meeting.

That is something conspicuously absent from the New Testament, both in precept and example. Therefore, it's important to look at the reason for this, and decide if what modern church goers generally experience is a necessary evolution toward a practiced and predictable worship experience, or rather a tragic manipulation of congregational dynamics. Is the useful, Spirit-empowered function of the people of God in the Christian gathering a thing of the past, no longer practicable in 21st century culture, or have we configured the assembly of saints in a way that essentially stifles the prerogatives of the Spirit through them? The question is as rhetorical as the answer is obvious.

I recently read an article quoting a source who instructs churches on worship service design, engineering programs that are both 'culturally relevant' and 'biblically faithful.' The latter element is certainly commendable, though I can barely relate to 'culturally relevant' as a requisite for *actual worship*. In my view, 'spiritually sensitive' might also be an important attribute in a gathering to entertain God's presence, though it requires more than a worship clinic to learn it. Obviously, the greater part of American Christianity is most comfortable ensuring a secure, relatively insulated platform for professional clergymen to direct well scripted 'worship' services, usually culminating in a 20 to 60 minute sermon of their choosing.

Before I continue, let me say that in all likelihood the people responsible for following the organizational model are well-intentioned. Many church leaders and pastors, whose character and service are admirable, nonetheless are among those who consistently suppress 'manifestations of the Spirit,' (1 Cor. 12:4-11; 14:22-26) in the church assembly, instead yielding to the constraints of the agenda, the clock, and the limited tolerance of a crowd conditioned to 90 minutes of seamless Christian programming.

In fact, what I call 'full-service Christianity' attempts to be a veritable casino of stimulus, entertainment, refreshment, enthusiastic celebration, and social interaction. There is lots of sound, and talk, and testimonials, and promotion; in some venues occasional pomp and pageantry. The organization strictly controls the environment. The layout of the building has everyone facing the platform, effectively saying to all that the agenda will originate at the front. The elevated platform (or the ascending seating) distinguishes the area of 'ministry' from the area of *non*-ministry. The relatively few but distinctive chairs at the front signals only select individuals may occupy them. On any given Sunday, enter a church and make your way forward and onto the platform . . . . *See what happens.*

These are all organizational issues; *form dictates function.* American Christianity has chosen to maintain traditional forms in order to facilitate predictable functions. They want folks to enter the church, take their seat in the congregation, and lend their vocal, physical, and financial 'Amen!' to everything that goes on.

And they try to script it so things are sharp and sequential, allowing everyone to get out on time.

The thing that is *not* supposed to happen is for some 'unapproved' individual to say or do something without prior consent. There is virtually no room for inspiration, revelation, or spontaneous anything. The deacons, the ushers, and in the case of larger venues, church security will quickly quash any attempt to 'interrupt' the program.

This is the accepted style of most Christian corporate function. It makes for a 'sanitized' religious regimen that the faithful may dutifully follow, and it allows visitors and the unchurched to 'get the feel' of church life and not encounter anything uncomfortable or controversial. Everybody wins.

Well, everyone except the Spirit of God, and the hungry, and the hurting. Please recall that this section began with Jesus' promise to be present whenever believers congregated in His name. The Apostles and the early church *expected* to be impacted by God's presence because of what they had witnessed in the ministry of Jesus, and the power and grace manifested at Pentecost. Jesus had fulfilled His promise to send the Holy Spirit among them, and it was generally expected that He would, in *some* way, replicate the presence of Jesus in word or deed through the assembled Spirit-filled believers.

"How is it then, brethren? Whenever you come together, each of you has a psalm, has a teaching, has a tongue, has a revelation, has an interpretation. Let all things be done for edification." (1 Corinthians 14:26 NKJV) Paul reminds the churches that there is a diversity of expressions and gifts that will be available for edification whenever the saints assemble. So he sets out some apostolic guidelines. What he clearly *does not do*, however, is enjoin leadership to suppress these expressions, but rather instructs leaders (pastors, prophets, apostles) in

how to channel them so they have a constructive outcome. (vs. 27-33) *"Do not quench the Spirit. Do not despise prophecies. Test all things; hold fast what is good."* (1 Thess. 5:19-21)

A ministry friend invited me to a teaching service in a nearby city. It was in a Women's Club facility seating about 200, and the room was packed. Arriving a bit late we sat near the back; I was stuck behind a huge man in a red plaid coat so I could barely see the speaker. I had never heard of him but the teaching was excellent and I was glad to receive some biblical encouragement. Jeanie and I were praying about launching a new ministry, so the blessing was appreciated.

Just as the speaker concluded his benediction he stepped into the aisle and began gesturing toward the back of the room. In a few moments it became evident he was pointing me out, though I wondered how he ever saw me. He asked me to stand and move to the aisle, and then began quietly speaking to me of the Lord's favor on my life and of the particular assignment the Lord was directing me toward. He listed my questions and concerns, and gave specific assurances of God's power and provision to address them. In some detail he declared how the Lord would bring about this blessing, and concluded by praying for its fulfillment.

As I sat down I was stunned by the clarity with which he spoke of conversations and issues only I could have known. The speaker? The pastor of a small local congregation, a man given to hearing and obeying the Spirit. For me that night, he was the voice of God, and every word of his prophecy was fulfilled within a year.

Strong apostolic and pastoral leadership is vital to the church but it's not easy. *"Freedom without chaos,"* is how Dr. Schaeffer used to describe the challenge of the church. Leaders must be ready to instruct, encourage, redirect, explain, and even rebuke if necessary, in order to guide the Christian gathering. Many leaders resist this role, choosing rather to orchestrate the agenda to avoid the inherent discomforts in hosting an open, Spirit-energized environment. I understand that discomfort, but that comes with the office. Leaders are the agents of Jesus Christ, commissioned to facilitate the Spirit's mind and heart toward, and through, the assembled believers.

Of course, conducting a meeting for a specific purpose such as a guest teacher, a clinic or seminar, or a concert is a blessing, and one that organized Christianity, with its larger venues, is better able to facilitate. I've found that the Spirit respects that intent (though some over-zealous believers do not), and moves the hearts and minds of the assembled in sync with the meeting's purpose.

However, the *worship gatherings* of the saints is another dynamic altogether, and I use the term 'dynamic' purposefully. When saints gather to worship God, that place becomes a junction of time and eternity and therefore, from our finite perspective, things may become more fluid than most of us are used to or comfortable with. There are three things I would offer about a corporate meeting with the Lord that may help inform and guide us. They are applicable whether the meeting is with 'two or three,' or three thousand.

1. The worship gathering is *for the Lord*, not for the people. Rather than being a form of religious expression or entertainment, it is a holy time when the saints *in fact* entertain the presence of God, and may expect to be personally engaged by Him.
2. Worship is, by definition, 'bowing the knee,' and whatever facilitates that in the hearts and minds of the assembled is appropriate. This may take the form of singing, prayer, concerted praise, the reading of scripture or liturgy, or silent reflection. Regardless of the form, it is a time to

individually and collectively present one's self to the Lord, and affirm one's affection and devotion to Him.

3. Worship always has a *destination*, and that destination is the living God, responding as a living being to His worshipping people. This may be experienced as a deepened sense of His presence, a reverence or awe within the people, or it may be manifested through spontaneous praise rising from the congregation. Sometimes spiritual gifts or spiritual songs may issue from the people, bringing insight, expressing adoration to God, or calling the saints to a deeper commitment to Him. At other times a leader may bring a prepared message which the Spirit affirms as God's voice to the people's hearts. Obviously, differing traditions and occasions lend to different responses. The important thing is that opportunity for, and sensitivity to, God's Spirit characterizes a leadership and a people mindful and respectful of His holy presence, and eager to receive what He has prepared for them.

Some Christians or groups might find what I've just described as strange; a bizarre sort of hyper-spirituality. They experience worship as a routine; a carefully crafted, doctrinally precise regimen which satisfies one's obligation to God, and salves the soul and conscience. That these folks are true Christians is not in question. Every person has the freedom to build his or her life on the foundation of faith in Christ as they perceive it. The fact remains, however, that the scriptures describe in rich detail the opportunity for every believer to enjoy a profoundly personal interaction with God in the gathering of saints as well as in the course of daily life. Jeanie and I have always tried to advocate for that.

When we organized Fayetteville Christian Fellowship in 1983 we had a two-fold objective. We prayed to create an environment of worship and freedom, with opportunity for a wide participation on the part of the believers, and we wanted to exalt Jesus Christ through the teaching of the scriptures. We instituted just enough organization to facilitate our objectives, and made this prayer / pledge to God and to ourselves; *"Put in place a structure that will essentially disintegrate without the immediate and sustained presence of the Holy Spirit in it."* In other words, if our practice is in any way inhospitable or insensitive to the Spirit, or if He is now moving in a different direction, let it expire. How faithfully we carried out that commitment only the Lord can judge, but that was our intention.

What is the point here? The Spirit-filled life produces a certain environment, first in one's heart, then in his home, and ultimately when he gathers with other people, saints or sinners. That environment creates the potential for kingdom transactions at any time, as the Spirit motivates His people. And that potential increases geometrically when a group of saints gather in Jesus' name. Therefore, believers who want to explore and enjoy the opportunity to personally experience God 'in the moment' should seek out other saints and leaders who value that very precious and potent environment more than the forms or prescriptions of a religious institution. *"Now the Lord is the Spirit, and where the Spirit of the Lord is, there is liberty – emancipation from bondage, freedom."* (2 Cor. 3:17 AMP)

A Parenthesis on the Time-Line – Acts 3:19
Jeanie and I personally witnessed a period of time, a decade more or less, in which the movements of God among a significant portion of the American church were so powerful and sovereign that the very memory of them is both a thrill and a heartache. What birthed it I can only speculate; prayer, hunger, repentance? Perhaps

just a Divine initiative. To enter a room full of believers was to feel breathless with anticipation. Sometimes it felt like an electric surge; a jolt in one's deepest parts. And with rare exceptions, one was never disappointed. People were converted, transformed, falling deeply in love with Jesus. It was invigorating to saints of nearly every tradition, many of them experiencing the moving and manifestations of the Spirit for the first time. It was an environment one never wanted to leave, or ever be without.

But within a few short years it had 'lifted,' for lack of a better word. That profound 'presence' of God was gradually (in some cases *suddenly*) replaced by a deep longing for more, and a hope, even a determination, to somehow see and feel it again. That was over 40 years ago in our experience, and only on rare occasions have we sensed anything quite like it again. I know individuals and entire groups from our generation who have traveled far and wide, hearing of something happening akin to their own experience, and hoping that the past was repeating itself. Most of those journeys, as I've visited with those who have undertaken them, failed to result in any lasting duplication of *'those days.'*

Many churches and ministries sprang up during the period I've just described, and when that great 'spiritual inertia' began to wane, lots of people were confounded and disillusioned, in the pulpits as well as the pews. What happens now? Everyone was scrambling to find 'the appropriate response' to a very challenging environmental vacuum, as far as our perceptions were concerned.

The approach of some was to artificially stimulate the church environment with lots of sounds and activities. Others simply retreated into the orthodoxies of their past, feeling it was a safe and prudent way to remain 'mainstream.' But still others, including Jeanie and me, began to practice *deliberately* the same things we had been doing *spontaneously*. We devoted more time to worshipping and praising the Lord, lifting our hands, singing in the Spirit (1 Cor. 14:15), and allowing space for the Spirit to manifest Himself through the believers present in exhortation, or bringing a prayer or song, or sometimes prophecy. Of course we continued to teach the scriptures, share the Lord's Supper, and minister to needs as the Lord and the Apostles instructed us to do.

What we learned from that remarkable season was considerable, and quite formative for our continued service to the Lord. First and foremost, we acknowledged the sovereignty of God; that He knows how to run His church, and at any time He has the right to move in and adjust things to His liking. (Matt. 16:18) As old Brother Hathcoat used to say, *"God can rule and overrule; God can take and undertake. God can work and none can hinder; God can hinder and none can work."* We decided to remember that every time we assembled with believers, and to make a place for His sovereign participation in and through the saints. We've surely not practiced that perfectly, but we've also never regretted the effort to keep that pledge.

We also learned that light can shine from any corner of the room, not just the platform. Ordinary believers were often inspired to pray, exhort, confront, prophesy, or lay hands on folks for special kinds of ministry and blessing. Insight and power is given *all the saints* through the Holy Spirit, and it was our calling to help facilitate that as much as possible within the bounds of order and mutual respect. For example, in our meetings with **The Antioch Group**, I'm usually in charge. But it is my responsibility to facilitate the Spirit's initiatives in the lives of those assembled. Leaders are present, as Jeanie puts it, *"to clear the coast for the Holy Ghost."* So we determined to value a wider participation of the saints in order to facilitate a more complete expression of the mind of the Spirit. (Romans 8:27)

And finally, we realized that individual Christians, or groups of believers, can become skillful in worship and entertaining the Lord's presence, helping to usher into the gathering a sense of 'sanctuary,' as Pastor Glenn Foster used to call it. Without instruction or coercion the people of God simply follow the prompting of the Spirit in praise, prayer, worship, and holy conversation, creating a 'unity of the Spirit' (Eph. 4:3) that may lead to further purposeful prayer, healing or miracles, a reverent silence, or simply a deep sense of satisfaction that we have honored and uplifted the name of the Lord.

Again, God's presence among His people always creates an *environment* for good, transforming things, and **You are the Plan** encourages every believer, under the Spirit's loving administration, to expect that he or she may, from time to time, have a part in it. It is fine to create a program designed to bless and instruct the saints. But when the environment moves us contrary to the program, it is better to move according to the Spirit. One gospel songwriter concluded a chorus with these profoundly simple lyrics; *"Let's determine in our hearts the way God's moving, and move with God."*

There is nothing extraordinary about this; 1 Corinthians 12 and 14 contain many of the necessary individual and collective guidelines for functioning this way. It is as Biblical as can be, but it requires a willing group of believers, experienced leaders, and a commitment to valuing the potential within Jesus' promise, *". . . . I am there in the midst of them."* (Matt. 18:20) And of course, positioned in the very heart of Paul's instruction is 1 Corinthians 13, standing watch over *all* Christian enterprise: *"Though I speak with the tongues of men and of angels, but have not **love**, I have become as sounding brass, or a clanging cymbal. . . ."*

We must be careful to not set ourselves in opposition to other rooms of the faith, or offer just another stylized template for

corporate Christian function. God forbid. It is awesome to contemplate the great diversity of the kingdom and the overarching
grace that allows us all to approach God through Christ, and not
through some religious 'needle's eye.' What we're setting out here
is *our* understanding and experience of the Biblical protocols, and
a vigorous encouragement of the saints to value a community of
freedom and function built on the foundation "which is Jesus
Christ." (1 Cor. 3:9-15)

10

A BRIEF WINDOW INTO 'THE MINISTRY'

Many pastors today do not shepherd most of their congregations; they preach to them and collect adulation and money from them.

The apostle Paul told the Ephesian believers that God has gifted the faith community with apostles, prophets, evangelists, pastors, and teachers *"for the equipping of the saints for the work of the ministry, for the building up of the Body of Christ."* (4:12) In other words, the saints will find among them those who are specially gifted in oversight, insight, foresight, communication and compassion, and their service to the Body will help everyone make a contribution to the strengthening and expansion of the faith.

Before we briefly reflect on these important gifts to the Church, let's review the context of this passage. *"There is one body and one Spirit, just as you were called in one hope of your calling; one Lord, one faith, one baptism; one God and Father of all, who is above all, and through all, and in you all. But to each one of us grace was given according to the measure of Christ's gift."* (Eph. 4:4-7)

Here Paul first affirms the solidarity of the Body of Christ, His church, and emphasizes that the Father is working in and through all of them. Obviously, each one's understanding and contribution varies "according to the measure of Christ's gift." But clearly a grace is upon *every* life to glorify Jesus Christ and bless others; a strategic truth that needs to be emphasized more strenuously and specifically in every Christian venue. And the end in view is *". . . till we all come to the unity of the faith and the knowledge of the Son of God, to a perfect (mature) man, to the measure of the stature of the fullness of Christ."* (vs. 13)

The "five-fold ministry," as it is sometimes called (apostles, prophets, pastors, etc.) is a unique population within the church. The Apostle Paul characterized his office as *"your servants for Jesus sake."* (2 Cor. 4:5) *"Who then is Paul, and who is Apollos, but ministers through whom you believed, as the Lord gave to each one? I planted, Apollos watered, but God gave the increase. So then neither he who plants is anything, nor he who waters, but God who gives the increase."* (1 Cor. 3:5-7) Much like the Levites in the Old Testament economy, who received no inheritance in Canaan (God said, *"I am your portion and your inheritance"* - Num. 18:20), the Apostle describes those in 'the ministry' as privileged to serve others on behalf of Jesus Christ, *"and each one will receive his own reward according to his own labor."* (1 Cor. 3:8) In other words, the ministry is special, but also *not* special.

American Christianity typically positions these ministry gifts somewhere within the institutional structure. Depending on the traditions we're discussing, pastors and teachers may be employees of a local church, or they may be bi-vocational; that is, serving a local congregation and also holding a secular job. Evangelists may work in, and travel out from, a local congregation, or they may be self-employed with their own ministry organization. Some Bible scholars link 'teachers' with pastors as a single gift, but I view teachers as a distinct ministry office.

Apostles and prophets, on the other hand, aren't even identifiable in many Christian groups. Some traditions use these titles to denote positions in their church hierarchy, or to describe a particular ministry expression in which one may function within that group. There are few scriptural examples of these ministry gifts within local congregations or the church at large, and the twelve Apostles which Jesus appointed were, in some ways at least, distinct from those who would subsequently be called apostles.

So, from a biblical standpoint, we have only a rather sketchy outline for how these ministry gifts serve the church. Even Peter and Paul said relatively little about them, except to set a high standard of personal and public conduct for 'elders,' and to encourage the saints to respect, appreciate, and compensate them for their service. The book of Acts and a couple of Paul's letters show the Apostles, or their close associates, appointing elders / pastors in various cities. Doubtless in some locations leaders 'emerged' from the local assembly of saints, recognized by everyone for the grace of God resting on them for leadership and gospel witness.

It has been interesting in 50 years to meet and observe many ministry people. I serve on the ordination council of a worldwide ministry organization, and have been involved in the oversight and formal recognition of hundreds of pastors, teachers, and evangelists. My association with them has been mostly positive and their fellowship rewarding. I've heard some great preachers (most of them you've never heard of), been in some churches that were genuine 'kingdom outposts,' and been moved by amazing works of compassion and care, both here and in other parts of the world. Praise God for the men and women who have devoted their lives to spreading the gospel, and bringing it to life through their service.

A couple of things are clear however. First, not everyone carrying the various titles given to the 'five-fold ministry' are actually gifts of Jesus Christ to the church. They may be talented, charismatic, and intelligent, but they clearly have an agenda quite their own. They may be building a kingdom, but mostly it's *not* the kingdom of God. Businessmen, entrepreneurs, entertainers, salesmen, and seducers have all made their way into the 'ministry,' and do outwardly impressive things. Church boards tend to like that. And too often the majority of folks in the pews don't know the difference. But the truth is, assuming a title doesn't mean one has been sent by God to the church. It shouldn't be considered disrespectful to be discerning.

The other thing I've observed is perhaps even more important to our purpose. I have met scores of individuals who have no position in the organized church at all, but are most definitely pastors, teachers, evangelists, etc. They may be store clerks or clerical workers, truck drivers, tradesmen, or teenagers; not matter, they help energize the body of Christ, bringing spiritual oversight, understanding, guidance, and the gospel within reach of those who need them. 1 Cor. 12:18 says, *"But now God has set the members, each one of them, in the body just as He pleased."* The Father knows where to put these folks to the greatest advantage for both the saints and the sinners.

The people in Jesus' day were confounded by the Apostles and the seventy Jesus sent out. Many of them were uneducated and unconnected, ordinary in every way. But the scripture says, *"They took note of them, that they had been with Jesus."* Their credentials and authority were an intimate knowledge of the Lord, and they were personally commissioned by Him. I suggest there are hundreds of thousands of just such people in our society today, commissioned and positioned by God. I have no problem calling them pastors or evangelists or whatever, based on their function, not on their association with a Christian organization.

Having said that, we should nonetheless maintain a deep appreciation for men and women of scholarship and discipline who have made great contributions to the church. Every time we pick up a concordance, a Greek dictionary, a commentary or devotional we're reminded that our kingdom efforts are built, to some extent, on the shoulders of diligent saints who have gone before us. I'm grateful for the insights and wisdom of dozens of scholars and teachers from numerous traditions that have made my service to the Lord easier, broader, and hopefully better.

In the past generation the institutional church has sometimes redefined for itself what the ministry gifts are, what they should be called, and how they should function. Institutions are free to do that, as they are created by people, and people usually like to leave their mark on things they've made. However, we're trying to reconcile what exists today with the biblical prototypes, and sometimes it's difficult to do. The biblical ministry titles (pastor, prophet, evangelist, elder) have rather clear meanings corresponding to calling, experience, gifting, or function. If these designations are changed, then at least the people being served should know what these new titles correspond to in scripture; what 'gift' of Jesus Christ they might be.

For example, in my understanding, *pastors touch people*. They know them and are known by them. They're available to them, sensitive to them, individually concerned about them. In the New Testament, the term 'pastor' is correspondent to 'shepherd,' *one who cares for a flock*, not merely feeding it. Peter charged some of the early Hebrew Christian elders to "shepherd the flock of God which is among you . . . . " (1 Peter 5:2)

Many 'pastors' today do not shepherd most of their congregations; they preach to them and collect adulation and money from them. They may only be visible on a large screen on the wall. They cannot be called on the phone, or contacted in any way by 'the sheep.' These individuals are not pastors to the greater part of their congregations. Yet the believers are expected to regard them as 'your pastor' when there is no biblical basis for it.

The shepherd who leaves the 99 to pursue the straying one is made to look rather pedestrian and antiquated by 'pastors' who jet around to their multi-campus churches delivering a polished 40 minutes of life-coaching wisdom. This new breed of pastors has no idea who is straying, praying, or decaying in their 'flock,' and that's not really their concern. Ecclesiastical executives, living in the rarified air of Christian media and celebrity, may be the stuff of the future for the updated American church . . . . but they may have little, or perhaps no commerce at all with the kingdom of God. Their value to the saints will be clarified on the Day of the Lord.

This is just one example of churches torqueing biblical terminology to serve more modernized structures, hierarchies and operational philosophies. The term 'deacon' is often used to denote members of a church board. 'Senior Pastor,' 'ruling elder,' 'preaching pastor,' 'life-coach,' care pastor,' etc. are all titles created to designate particular functions in organized Christianity, which don't clearly correspond to the biblical examples. Nevertheless, change is inevitable in the realm of human beings, and institutional churches, as one of the prominent sociological structures in our society, will doubtless continue to modernize their terminology to keep pace with the cultural rhythms of their populations.

What is important for the saints, however, is the ability, and actually the *right*, to be able to identify those 'gifts' whom God has positioned in the church by the Spirit's sovereign administration. Why is this important? Because those are the folks we all rely on to be *"examples to the believers in word, in conduct, in love, in spirit, in faith, in purity."* (1 Tim. 4:12) As I observe the trends in contemporary Christianity, I recall one scholar's rendering of Matthew 24:35; *"Heaven and earth shall move with the times, but My words will not move with the times."* While many biblical terms and practices are being bulldozed by parts of contemporary Christianity, it will always be important for God's people to identify those things which should be regarded as landmarks, and therefore preserved. (Proverbs 22:28)

Growing up in mostly traditional Evangelicalism I encountered many pastors and leaders, most of whom made a positive contribution to my understanding and faith. But along the journey I also was deeply impacted by other believers whose gifts and character made me pause, and then recognize that God had placed them in strategic ministry positions as truly as the folks filling pulpits on Sunday mornings.

The conclusion here is rather simple; continue to respect and value those who are faithfully leading and instructing the traditional churches, but also expect to find genuine ministry gifts strategically 'sown' throughout the Body of Christ. There's no need to catalogue them in a systemic, or organizational way. That only suggests another hierarchy, and fails to validate Jesus' word that *"whoever desires to become great among you shall be your servant."* (Matt. 10:27; Mark 10:43) Most religious institutions will continue to emphasize the 'graded positions' within the organization, but **You are the Plan** suggests we may also celebrate the ministry of those 'servant saints' hidden away in schools, shops, factories, and office complexes, precisely where the battle lines are drawn.

11

KEEPING IT REAL

It is sad when we make decisions about people based more on their affiliations than by the look in their eye, or a sense of their spirit.

"We should measure ourselves by the amount of peace and freedom the people who fellowship with us actually walk in." My son Michael and I were reflecting on the number of professing Christians we know who, while good folks, are not at peace in themselves, and are not truly free people. His statement suggested a rather rigorous way of evaluating ourselves and our influence. What can we do to promote peace and freedom in others? Certainly we can begin by challenging some of the things that create division, prejudice, and bondage.

As most of us have experienced, relationships with other saints can be a huge source of encouragement, fortification, and joy. I have such fond memories of many great saints having a part in our lives as I was growing up, and in the fifty plus years Jeanie and I have served the Lord together. The New Testament is filled with references to, and examples of men and women 'being there' for one another, demonstrating the love Jesus asked us to freely give; the marker that would distinguish us as His followers. (John 13:35) Our challenge is to embrace all the believers on the level that Jesus did; that is, love for the person apart from the myriad of social and religious models that categorize and separate.

Much of traditional Christianity brings people together around a doctrine or creed, a social agenda, a personality, or an experience of some kind. That's why they put signs out front that say more than 'church.' They either put up the denominational marker (i.e. Methodist, Adventist, Pentecostal, etc.) or they try to describe themselves with words like Life, or Unity, or Love, or Freedom, or Holiness. Of course, that's fine; it lets folks passing by apply a certain filter to their decision whether or not to venture inside.

Besides presenting literally hundreds of denominations and sub-groups, American Christianity also has a full complement of labels for assignment to people's beliefs, practices, taboos, and traditions. Labels like liberal, fundamentalist, holy roller, social gospel, clothes-line saints, born agains, hate-mongers, small minded, crazy creationists, progressive, word of faith, sipping saints, high church, end-of-the-worlders, tangent group, sloppy agape; on and on it goes. I suppose these markers are considered useful in defining and defending a group's distinctive character by having a handy classification for those who aren't like them. In my experience they're often employed in a conversation purportedly about *sound doctrine.*

The problem with these labels is the stifling, confining attitude they produce within many Christians, and Christian organizations, reducing the formation of relationships to a 'paint-by-numbers' business. *"Entertain no one outside these lines!"* On top of that, relationships within traditional church structures are sometimes difficult to gain simply because the usual paradigm for Christian gatherings doesn't really lend itself to it. Folks file in and file out. It's no one's 'fault;' unless you go out of your way to engage people, sitting in rows facing the front doesn't facilitate much interaction.

I recently had a couple of conversations with some young believers, both of whom had been looking for somewhere to go to church. Each of them shared their difficulty in really *connecting* with anyone over the months they'd been attending. The greeters welcomed them in the door, but almost no one else made any attempt to approach them. I've heard that sentiment from scores of people over the years, and it makes you wonder how that degree of fear or backwardness persists in so many professing Christian populations.

A church in my area recently sent out a letter to all the attendees advising them on the appropriate way to dress for their services. That particular group was a bit older and relatively affluent, so their concern was obviously for the continued viability of their preferred, and more comfortable, public presentation. And many groups actually canonize these kinds of regulations so that if excommunication should become necessary, it would never be messy or appear arbitrary, but would be based on something substantial; an *ecclesiastical document!*

To the point, it's a really risky business to base our relationships with believers on shared doctrines, or creeds, or words with certain connotations. If you do, then that's a pretty vulnerable relationship. The moment you don't live up to the expectations of the person or group, either doctrinally or in 'approved' practice, you're in a jam. You can suddenly, almost miraculously become a non-person, even a heretic; now regarded very differently than you were the previous day. Incidents of this kind are of course legendary in every sector of organized Christianity; often devastating to the individual singled out, but usually leaving the folks in the organization feeling more pristine and whole.

This is not to say doctrine (or perhaps we should call it 'sound teaching') is not important. Paul urged young Timothy to *"be diligent to present yourself approved to God, a worker who does not need to be ashamed, rightly dividing the word of truth."* (2 Tim. 2:15) But it is love and devotion to Jesus Christ that is truly essential in our faith, and a shared commitment to Him is the foremost bond of Christian fellowship. We can spend a lifetime debating doctrine, but our 'love of the brethren' rests on a simple distinction between life and death. *"He who believes in the Son has everlasting life, and he who does not believe the Son shall not see life . . ."* (John 3:36)

Many church organizations carry on a love affair with words. The conviction seems to be the more they're able to itemize, categorize, and systematize their beliefs, practices, and standards the better. Not only do they produce very sophisticated doctrinal statements but they also create documents of policy, procedure, and protocol for almost every part of church life. The problem with this glut of words is how quickly they associate themselves with individuals. Soon they may become labels, barriers, or boxes which efficiently compartmentalize people, strangling uniqueness, creativity, and ultimately relationship.

The calculated manipulation of words in media is an obvious example of a wider problem in our society, including the church. Rather than being tools of clarification and unification, words are frequently used to evoke responses and shape behaviors. I'm not talking about preaching the gospel, but about *sectarian propaganda.* It's especially evident in politics and commerce, but the churches often follow suit; instead of using words to bring people in rhythm with the heart of God, they're used to bring them into step with a particular viewpoint, and its supporting agenda. Words are surely useful to clarify a position, but they can quickly solidify into law. Words are *weapons*; they can set off shockwaves of prejudice and division.

When individuals become part of an institutional church, in reality they are unwittingly assigned (and accepting) some sort of label, or labels; unstated assumptions about what they believe, what they endorse, how they live, and to some degree what they *are*. Christians meeting for the first time, for example, find themselves asking the other party, "Well, *what are you?*" In other words, what is your denominational/doctrinal label? While it is understandable, particularly in American Christian culture, it can immediately put the relationship on a 'Jesus, plus some other stuff,' basis.

Labels create separation and discrimination, and believers involved in institutional Christianity will be perceived in various ways simply because of their association with it. Of course, many professing Christians don't care about this at all, or haven't even given it a thought. But the fact is, when we adopt a label (a religious description), our liberty in Christ has, in many instances, taken on well-defined limits and has become subject to scrutiny and expected compliance. Granted, some people might call this 'accountability,' and that's not a bad thing unless and until it limits our freedom to explore, and question, and think, and 'grow in the grace and knowledge of our Lord and Savior Jesus Christ.' (2 Peter 3:18)

Wherever one chooses to serve the Lord, whether in a traditional church context or some other Christian venue, personal freedom for the individual believer requires a careful, consistent *disassociation* from the labels, and an identification only with Jesus Christ. However impractical and idealistic that may sound, it is where we need to purposely, publicly, and steadfastly stand. We're part of a kingdom represented, not by a doctrine or tradition, but by a Life. As such, our doctrine, our catechism, our standard is the person of Jesus Christ.

That's a demanding position to maintain, but by insisting on it for ourselves (and to anyone else who is interested) we free ourselves from a divided loyalty. We may be loyal to *other saints*, as fellow human beings and followers of Jesus, but our loyalty is not to an institution. That doesn't mean we're not supportive of its positive attributes; it simply means that the organization and its corresponding label(s) don't represent us. We participate as free souls, and we haven't signed anything that says, "Now, *this* is what I am."

At the same time, we should offer the same courtesy to other saints. *It is sad when we make decisions about people based more on their affiliations than by the look in their eye, or a sense of their spirit.* We don't need a theologian to decide if we're to love someone or not. Our kingdom commitment must be to *people,* not to an organization, list, or lineup of some kind. That's why the parable of the Good Samaritan is so valuable to us. He didn't at all fit the accepted profile, but he did the God-thing! He's the guy who will 'be there for you' just because you're a *person.* Who does that sound like?

Again, fellowship (much less real community) can't be based on words; that is, doctrine or theology. It must be based on *experience.* Words *about me,* or about what I purportedly believe, will never communicate *ME* to you. Only listening to me and being with me can do that. This is true not only of people, but also of God. Beliefs *about* God can never fully communicate God to us; we must seek Him, engage Him, and listen to Him before our knowledge will find a firm footing.

Perhaps it will help when we understand that much of what the scriptures contain is 'meta-data,' that is, information that facilitates the discovery of other relevant things. When we read the words of Isaiah; *"In the year that king Uzziah died, I saw the Lord sitting on a throne, high and lifted up, and the train of His robe filled the temple . . ."* (Is. 6:1), we're not actually experiencing what Isaiah did, but we're getting his best effort to communicate his experience to us. The value of this account is surely great, because it directs our souls toward something; an anticipation that God is *really there*, and we too may personally encounter Him.

The fact remains, however, that we may read this account dozens of times without ever having an experience with God. The words contain valuable information that can help move us toward something, but they are not 'the thing' itself. Encountering God is what we're after. However, *by over-valuing knowledge of the words*, some Christian groups unwittingly divert many believers from the actual experience the words describe. I've known professed believers who can quote vast portions of the scriptures but you have trouble connecting with the Spirit of the Lord in them. They acquire an intimate knowledge of the map, but never reach the destination! (Hosea 6:3)

I've used the term 'Word worship' for this vigorous promotion of scriptural and doctrinal acumen at the expense of relationship. (James 2:19) Perhaps unintentionally, God's voice is confined to paper and text, requiring 'qualified' authorities to bring enlightenment and corporate approval within reach of the ordinary folks. That's what is known as 'religion!' Nevertheless, whether it is with God or men, *relationship is the 'thing,' and the value of the Word and all good teaching is that it moves us steadily toward deeper communion with God and more meaningful relationships with people.*

Of course we should distance ourselves from individuals whose behavior and language are violent, seductive, dishonest, or blasphemous. But even Jesus was sometimes seen with folks who were not 'approved' by the religious establishment. Frankly, believers who never have a meaningful relationship with a nonbeliever or two often draw uninformed, and sometimes silly conclusions about what motivates those around them, and what they're thinking. We might avoid that if we take to heart the observation made about some modern theologians; "It's not that they don't have the answers; *they don't know the questions!*" In the real world, it's not our knowledge that draws folks to us, but their conviction that *we really hear them.*

Religion tends to use its own vocabulary, but healthy relationships with saints and sinners must be carried on in every day, real world terminology. The impact of our witness depends heavily on the soundness of our humanity; living faithfully, day in and day out, as everyone else has to live. We should also give those in relationship with us the freedom to be a creature before God on their own terms. Their development as a person in Christ will, in some ways, be much different than our own. It is precisely at that point that we must be careful not to label, or categorize them as this or that. Our part in their lives is not to conform them to a particular spiritual viewpoint or practice, but to encourage them, along with us, to vigorously pursue a relationship with Jesus. Again, institutions tend to value conformity, but the saints appreciate God's rich diversity in human beings.

Some kind of religious affiliation is not a kingdom demand. *Identification* with Jesus Christ and His people *is.* We are challenged to develop godly relationships ('kingdom connections,' we might call them) which transcend sectarian divisions so the witness of "one Lord, one faith, one baptism" can reach those who very much need to see it. Again, more words will not aid us in this task.

Jeanie and I have met thousands of Christian individuals in our lifetime, and we're blessed that some of them became a cherished, and often strategic part of our journey. Some were affluent, some were poor; some educated and others not. Many shared our viewpoint on most things, but others had quite different views on many issues. Some were Republicans, others were Democrats, and quite a few didn't participate. But we *knew* them, and came to value their realness, their integrity, and their devotion to the interests of Jesus Christ.

When folks are in agreement about Jesus, and enjoy the unique and rich texture He brings to a relationship, their differences in philosophy and doctrine are surprisingly easy to subordinate to the greater blessing of real brotherhood and fellowship. That makes the journey sweeter and the reality of the gospel clearer for everyone.

12

YOU ARE THE PLAN

> Our defining desires will always be an important
> part of our life of faith, and they rarely diminish or
> change very much.

'From complexity toward simplicity; from bondage toward freedom." Earlier
I stated this as a guiding principle for evaluating the trajectory of
our spiritual journey. Now I want to set out some things that com-
mend **You are the Plan** to both our reason and biblical understanding. In keeping with our stated principle, they are relatively
simple (though not necessarily easy), and they lead toward *freedom*.

You are the Plan states in plain language God's blueprint for
your future. You are unconditionally loved and valued, and He has
chosen you, called you, and put His Spirit in you by His own will,
and for His good pleasure. He understands your limitations but
He has His eye on some rich deposits within you that you've yet to
fully discover or acknowledge. He has ushered your life back to
the simplicity of Eden's garden, where God walked and communed
with man in an unhurried and most personal way. His priorities

are relational; His plans, and yours, are mutually discovered and carried out. There is no compulsion. Only the quiet sharing of life, human and Divine, which in its progress and development will take its rightful place in the great chronicle of redemption.

It is God's intention for *every truly converted believer* to play a meaningful role in His kingdom economy. The *measure* of that role only God knows. Some individuals or groups may *appear* to have greater significance than others, but the scriptures, and particularly the words of Jesus, assure us that things as simple as giving a cup of water in His name are noteworthy acts commanding Divine recognition. (Mark 9:41) *"She has put in more than everyone else,"* Jesus declared as the widow cast her pennies in the temple treasury. (Luke 21:1-4) I believe He meant it! Sadly, the prevalent business/success model embraced by much of the American Church blinds many to the Divine viewpoint.

> *"No Christian has a special work to do. A Christian is called to be Jesus Christ's own . . . . Our Lord calls to no special work: He calls to Himself."*
>
> —Oswald Chambers

It is important to recall God's 'original intent' for creation, and particularly for human beings. The biblical record shows Adam and Eve were given simple instruction to be fruitful and fill the earth and subdue it. Adam was never challenged to be successful, or to build himself an empire. He was only told to 'cultivate and keep' the place where he was. In much the same way, we've been given the freedom to develop a life as we feel motivated inside. God's Spirit oversees our thoughts, our desires, and our plans, inviting us to fully appreciate *His* thoughts regarding us. (Psalm

139:17, 18; Jeremiah 29:11) In a most unconscious and seamless way, the Holy Spirit blends the flow of God's purposeful intent with our conscious stream of thought, daily, even hourly, gently and steadily influencing us toward 'The Highway' where no one goes astray. (Isaiah 35:8)

Interestingly, in the entire Sermon on the Mount, recognized as some of the highest moral teaching written, not a word is said about carrying out those teachings in a *corporate* church context. The only references in Matthew 5-7 that might suggest a public setting are, *"Beware of false prophets who come to you in sheep's clothing"* (7:15), and *". . . unless your righteousness exceeds the righteousness of the scribes and Pharisees, you will by no means enter the kingdom of heaven."* (5:20) Even the call to prayer, fasting, and charitable giving was spoken with the encouragement to perform them secretly, *"that your Father who sees in secret will Himself reward you openly."* (6:4, 6, 18)

What this suggests is that Jesus' teaching was directed toward ordinary men and women, equipping them to live godly, honorably, and peaceably with family and neighbors, bearing witness to God's presence, grace, and glory through the daily exercises all human beings share. When believers grasp that the plan of God consists of the collective thoughts, intentions, visions, plans, prayers, and consequent actions of all the saints as they respond moment to moment to the Spirit's leading, the Christian life takes on a different character. We are not hobbled by trying to figure out some *result* that God wants from us. We are freed to live deliberately and passionately, doing the 'thing at hand' and leaving the result to Him. He will employ our eager and obedient action, and that of others, to work "all things according to the counsel of his will." (Ephesians 1:11) He knows how.

When Jesus gazed at the masses on the hills and meadows of Judea, the Bible records that He was moved with compassion for them, for *'they were like sheep without a shepherd.'* So then, as the Good Shepherd, what kind of care and provision did He have in mind for them? Was it the religious activity we see around us; in general, Sunday morning gatherings and the host of other activities common to American Christianity? As valuable as those may be, they fall far short of His abundant supply.

Jesus' vision for them was universal in scope yet profoundly simple. Deposit the Spirit of His Father in every man and woman so that each may uniquely receive and reflect God's character, and experience His presence and power right there where life happens, where hunger and thirst is greatest. And the Good Shepherd will not only lead them; He will be *"with them and in them."*

Jesus produced no outline or organizational plan for His disciples to follow after He was gone. That was not the platform His kingdom would be founded on. (Eph. 2:19-22) The Apostles, of course, had to deal with a Christian population that was expanding rapidly (Acts 2:41; 4:4; 6:1), and much of the New Testament outlines a practical framework and directives for fellowship, leadership, service, and corporate worship. However, the emergence of 'Christianity' (Acts 11:26) as a corporate social entity was an 'effect' of the Spirit's movements among the multitudes; it would be a mistake to regard it as a 'cause.' In God's economy, Kingdom activity produces and feeds the church community, not the other way around.

It's also a curious fact, as I stated before, Jesus made no attempt to transform or reconfigure ceremonial Judaism. Instead He chose to arrest the most rabid and radical personality *within* Judaism; a Pharisee whose zeal had ignited into a murderous violence, and *transform him.* Saul of Tarsus became the living example of how God would get things done; *use the people!* (Acts 9:1-31)

Person by person, whether Peter, or Stephen, or Paul, Aquila and Priscilla, Barnabus, Timothy, James or John, the Spirit empowered individuals to vividly proclaim and demonstrate the kingdom of God. Yet it goes without saying that these individuals, whose names made it into Luke's record of the early church, were a handful among tens of thousands of other Christians whose words and actions gave greater traction to the movement of the gospel around the known world. And still today, it is that vast ocean of redeemed souls that supports the great tide of God's redemptive activity.

Doubtless God has human history on track to fulfill His ultimate purposes, but we don't know very many details about that. Folks have been using the Revelation, Matthew 24, and Daniel to piece together, like a spiritual jigsaw puzzle, the culmination of history. Despite these efforts, though, the only thing that's *clear* about any of it is the outcome; God's ultimate triumph over evil, sin, and death through the sacrifice and resurrection of His Son. Everything else is speculation.

Nevertheless, setting 'end-of-the-age' time lines, making predictions, and producing publications is a thriving industry in evangelical Christian culture. Unfortunately it is often counterproductive to kingdom interests by diverting believers toward what is peripheral and speculative and away from where Jesus asked us to direct our attention;

"It is not for you to know times and seasons which the Father has put in His own authority. But you shall receive power when the Holy Spirit has come upon you; and you shall be witnesses to Me in Jerusalem, and in all Judea and Samaria, and to the end of the earth." (Acts 1:7, 8)

In other words, Jesus deflected the disciples' focus away from concern for the future, and onto the awesome journey they had begun; accepting a functioning part in the company of saints who would spread His 'good news' throughout the earth. The early disciples did precisely that, and became those who, in the minds of the Thessalonians at least, *'turned the world upside down.'* (Acts 17:6)

Toughing it out

"Our whole life is startlingly moral. There is never an instant's truce between virtue and vice."

—Thoreau; Walden

I can imagine more than one good soul saying, *"Roger, this all has a nice sound to it, but the truth is, I have some real problems in my head and my heart!"* In a perfect world all of us would be highly competent, well adjusted, profoundly spiritual, and issue free. Obviously, that's not the case. So far from feeling like "the plan," many Christians struggle with life's most basic transactions from time to time, and can easily feel disqualified from the kingdom participation we've been describing. The good news is, God isn't shocked by our inadequacies.

When I stand before a gathering of believers for the first time I will often tell them, *"You're the best God's got!"* The grammar isn't great but the truth of it surely is. All He has to work with is people, and all of us are so ordinary in most ways. However, living in union with Jesus will *always* yield some good things, both in us and around us. (John 15:4, 5) *More good news*; none of us has a quota!

The Christian life is not a contest; all that kind of devastating requirements were finished at the cross. (Coll. 2:14) We are all just 'laborers in His vineyard,' and He's going to evaluate, appreciate, and compensate us *individually*, as it pleases Him. *"Whatever is right you will receive!"* (Matt. 20:1-16) We may be sure *that's* good news too!

All of us share in the conflict between what we aspire to and what we're actually able to do. Our vision is often greater than our reach. Disappointment is a killer, and it's especially tough when we've disappointed ourselves. Things we thought we could make happen didn't, and other stuff did. We were mistaken, or we miscalculated, or we were just plain stupid. This is all common in the human experience, and Christians participate equally in it. How liberating it is to discover that even such distressing times will likely become a strategic part of our journey when we fully apprehend the scope and beauty of **You are the Plan**.

There is much in all of us that confounds and frustrates. *"For the flesh lusts against the Spirit, and the Spirit against the flesh, and these are contrary to one another, so that you do not do the things that you wish."* (Gal. 5:17) Paul was very forthright about the human condition; his and everyone else's. The remedy, however, is right there in the surrounding verses; *"Walk in the Spirit . . . if you are led of the Spirit, you are not under the law."* (Gal. 5:16, 18) The answer to the dilemma of our humanity is not sophisticated or complex, it's just challenging, demanding. We must cast our broken humanity upon Him, and by the faith He gives us through His Spirit, eagerly lay claim to His righteousness as our own. (Phil. 3:8, 9; Eph. 2:8, 9) It is at once a most humbling and exhilarating transaction!

God intends for us to be comfortable with our humanity, despite its many areas of weakness, for *"As a Father pities his children, so the Lord pities those who fear Him. For He knows (understands) our frame; He remembers that we are dust."* (Psalm 103:13, 14) He is not put off by our occasional silliness, or weirdness, or when we're clueless. That is the very reason He has given us His Spirit! *"Likewise the Spirit also helps in our weaknesses . . . . the Spirit Himself makes intercession for us . . . . according to the will of God"* (Romans 8:26, 27)

We're going to make mistakes, take some wrong turns; we can count on it. But those mistakes will not be our undoing as we keep holding to His righteousness, acknowledging our blunders, and *stay in the game!* After all, *if we pull out,* who's going to take our place? We're the one God has deposited strategically within a certain human context, and we're the best He has *in this place, at this time!* Like my friend Gary Szmyd told a men's group one evening, sharing about the challenges of the Christian journey; "Hey man, no matter how you think you're doing, *you've gotta participate!*" That continues to be a valuable kingdom perspective! *"All things* (the good, and the not-so-good) *work together for good to those who love God, who are the called according to His purpose."* (Romans 8:28)

We are never, ever to despise our human-ness! After all, the Lord knows what it's like to journey in human flesh, and He is, in His glorified humanity, now seated in the place of greatest authority; at His Father's right hand. Because of that we are afforded a dignity and self-worth in our humanity that was gained by the shedding of His precious blood. Christian men and women are not challenged to be 'spiritual specimens' for others to admire, but rather living examples of God's mercy, grace, and love applied to a needy soul. We can *do that!*

As we seize this glorious challenge, we must also be careful to think corporately. **You are the Plan** does not suggest we are somehow quite self-sufficient, and that there is little need for godly relationships, Christian community, or spiritual leadership. These are all important ingredients of a healthy life in the Lord. The blessing of wise, experienced counsel, godly encouragement, and folks who will speak the truth to us cannot be overestimated. Many of these blessings may indeed be found among those saints within the church institutions. However, it's important to *begin* at the place where God begins, in our own heart. (Coll.1:27) That's where He meets us, and all spiritual life issues from there.

The Administrator, the Holy Spirit, will always be working to create vital kingdom connections between us and the believers around us, generating fellowship, mutual instruction, accountability, and service in the churches and beyond them. His leadership from within always directs us toward a healthy relation to everything outside ourselves. "Abundant life" is what Jesus came to provide for us (John 10:10), so we may expect God's grace to bring us some friends, some mentors, some adversaries, some opportunities, and some challenges, all mixed together in a most curious way to ultimately produce good things, both *for* us and *through* us.

Down the Road

As I shared before, the Spirit spoke these words inside me; *"The present forms of Christianity are not adequate for the twenty-first century."* Since then I've been looking for clarification and direction from within, and for other witnesses to that word among the saints. The challenges ahead will doubtless be great and some of them will be without precedent. For that reason we may expect the Lord to enhance our ability to adapt to rapid cultural and environmental changes. The gospel, too, is very fluid; its timeless content will always match the contour of every human need, in every period on the time-line.

Technology assures us of an ever-increasing dependence on things we don't understand and cannot control. The sheer quantity of information flowing through the culture promises a more complex maze of data-driven politics, economics, and education. Entrenched evolutionary theory demands that traditional ideas and institutions make way for more progressive perspectives on ethics, morality, and religion. And the increasing tension between our western democracy and the rapid rise of Eastern fundamentalism is beginning to challenge our customary and comfortable way of life in new, unanticipated ways. The world, and our culture along with it, is significantly mutating under these influences, and if present trends continue, fewer people are going to be genuinely transformed and equipped by simply 'going to church.'

Do these challenges threaten the general effectiveness of the gospel? Absolutely not. But they *do* present issues for individuals and groups who are sustained only by a rigid, ritualistic, doctrinally driven religious practice. Simply embracing certain cherished forms and beliefs will not insulate the soul and spirit from *"the rulers of the darkness of this age."* (Eph. 6:12) At some point their spiritual applecart will likely be upset as they find themselves surrounded and infiltrated by potent forces that don't play fair or clean, leaving them conflicted or confused. Desperate parishioners will wilt and wither for a lack of real spiritual nourishment. Many of these folks will simply maintain their religious forms but will have little energy, or even concern for kingdom significance. But some, by the grace of God, may battle to regain their 'kingdom orientation,' and bear good fruit.

However, one thing I'm confident the twenty-first century *will see* is the resurgence of a *Jesus movement*; a tide of Spirit-energized people who have seized ownership of the gospel and have accepted their calling to walk out *'The Plan.'* Both within the churches and in the holy routine of Christian homes, families, and social interaction, the saints will effectively carry the message and ministry of Jesus to friends, family, and beyond under the loving guidance of the Holy Spirit. So, our purpose now is to help and encourage these believers to fulfill this calling in a kingdom climate alive with *"righteousness, and peace, and joy in the Holy Spirit."* (Romans 14:17)

Benchmarks

The things that influence how the saints choose to live are varied and complex, but I'm briefly highlighting three that are most foundational in walking out **You are the Plan**. First, and most obvious, our responsibilities and integrity, then the leading of the Holy Spirit, and finally our inner desires and motivations. Again, because we live in a time when almost every believer in our culture has a copy of the scriptures, it is assumed that all three of these areas will be continually informed by our eager attention to the Bible. *"If you know someone whose Bible is falling apart, you probably know someone who isn't!"*

1. For all human beings, life mostly consists of doing the necessary things; the things that keep everything going for us and for our families, and the things that integrity demands. These include a wholesome attitude, doing some good, productive work, reliability toward one's family, and uprightness in one's interaction with society. In these the Lord expects us to be diligent and consistent, and most folks would agree that we need the Lord's strength to help us persevere in these mundane aspects of life. And it's in these things, perhaps more than anywhere, that our character is revealed and refined, and our qualification for Christian service enlarged.

   Everyone is born into a unique cultural setting, both geographically and within one's family. The political, economic, and religious dynamics of these diverse cultural influences will impact us deeply, and often will challenge the truth of Jesus' gospel, and the Lord's place in our lives. Consequently, the task of living truthfully, honestly, and honorably amid the ferment of many adverse perspectives will be perhaps our most significant kingdom assignment.

   Portions of the scriptures, like any history, sometimes distort the picture for us by recording only the highlights of a particular life or journey, often omitting months, years, or even decades between significant incidents. The ancient saints did a lot of living between those recorded events and miracles! Honing a skill or trade, helping one's neighbors, acquiring needed stuff, fixing the broken stuff, giving birth to one's children, traveling to a distant land, battling for a yield from a piece of ground, enduring years of unchanging labor; these are all things we do to survive, and to provide stability and definition for our lives. Sure, they would likely be just the *footnotes* to our memoirs, but they were what consumed most of our time! Faith and perseverance are both indispensable in the daily life of a Christian. (Heb. 6:12; 12:1)

2. The leadership of the Holy Spirit (Romans 8:14; Galatians 5:16-18) is a precious privilege for every Christian. Jesus of Nazareth demonstrated for all believers the compatibility of one's humanity with the Spirit of God, beginning with His baptism. (Matt. 3:16) The Apostle Paul's letter to the Ephesians records a couple of prayers for the saints, one which included the remarkable phrase, "... *that you may be filled with all the fullness of God.*" (Eph. 3:19) It is the Lord's good purpose to live in union with us, and to influence our journey from the inside!

   However, the presence and work of the Holy Spirit in our lives is rather challenging to talk about in categorical terms, because everyone apprehends and responds to the Holy Spirit differently. I'm offering here a very brief, general, and doubtless subjective description of the Spirit-led life .... and may I say quickly, I'm definitely not the poster child for this, even after more than 50 years.

   This is also a subject about which we must be open, charitable, and not dogmatic in our discourse with believers outside our traditions. Every group defines or describes the Spirit's activity in terms, and by examples that are quite often peculiar to that group. For one tradition spirituality is, in general, a matter of religious instruction, doctrine, and intellect; for another it may be quite different; more experiential, subjective, and engaged with the emotions.

The essential thing for our purpose is not the terminology or template we employ in describing the Spirit and His work, but the acknowledgement of His immediate presence, and a diligent, prayerful attentiveness to His purposeful movements in and through us. *"Be (continually) filled with the Spirit,"* Paul urged the saints. (Eph. 5:18)

The scriptures affirm, as we stated earlier, that the Spirit is a person, and regardless of how one prefers to explain the relationship of Father, Son, and Holy Spirit, I'm satisfied to simply regard Him as the Spirit of Jesus (Romans 8:9). It is the Spirit who fulfills Jesus' promise, *"I am with you always, even to the end of the age."* (Matt. 28:20) As Charles Spurgeon put it, "The one thing we know *for sure* is that He is with us!"

When Paul told the Galatians to *"Walk in the Spirit,"* he was talking about a way of life; a conscious attentiveness to our inner selves. Saints in the Philippines used to refer to the Spirit within as 'the resident boss.' The union of the Holy Spirit with our spirit makes communion with God an internal, very private business. In Greek, the language of the New Testament, the word for spirit, wind, and breath are the same. His presence is hardly distinguishable from our own 'aliveness;' His movements and stirrings are unpredictable, sometimes subtle, sometimes powerful, like the wind. (John 3:8) Because of this, we must maintain an openness in our souls to His stirrings. Absorbing the scriptures is so valuable in this process because *they sound like Him.* We discover over time that the Spirit and the Word are always working to find each other within us, and help bring resolution to any recurring dissonance in our daily experience, both internal and external. (1 John 5: 6, 7)

Perhaps the best word in common usage to describe how we sense the mind of the Spirit is 'intuition.' That is, we experience a 'knowing' about a matter that does not come to us through the normal rational process. Watchman Nee, the great Chinese Christian of the 1930's, taught his disciples to listen for *'the soundless, unuttered voice'* of the Holy Spirit. He, too, described this communication of the Spirit as 'intuition.' (The Spiritual Man, Vol 2, pp. 70-72)

"The Spirit Himself bears witness with our spirit that we are children of God..." (Romans 8:16). At the very outset of our journey with the Lord the Spirit begins to 'testify' within us of realities that cannot be apprehended rationally. Most of us recall when we were converted (born again) by faith in Christ we immediately realized our vital connection to God; we 'knew' we had *"passed from death into life."* (Matt. 5:24) *"For our gospel did not come to you in word only, but also in power, and in the Holy Spirit, and in much assurance...."* (1 Thess. 1:5) Here Paul declares that God's voice is accompanied by an affirming inner witness to Jesus' presence and involvement with us. Just as the Lord promised, the Spirit will faithfully *"take of what is Mine, and declare it unto you."* (John 16:14; 1 Cor. 2:9-12)

The regenerated human spirit, that *eternal* part of us, receives information and impressions at a different, deeper

level than the mind; a communication that warmly resonates with *"eternity in (our) hearts."* (Ecc. 3:11) The longer we
walk with the Lord the more we become aware of that distinctive voice. Pastor Nee also taught believers to rely on
the word of God to further clarify the Spirit's expressions;
*"For the word of God is living and powerful, and sharper than any
two-edged sword, piercing even to the division of soul and spirit, and of
joints and marrow, and is a discerner of the thoughts and intents of the
heart."* (Hebrews 4:12) This familiar passage suggests the
more we expose ourselves to the living scriptures the more
discerning we become about the source of every thought;
from our mind or spirit.

How do we develop this sensitivity? We prayerfully
and consistently practice it. Western Christianity, and
Protestantism in particular, doesn't usually emphasize the
disciplines of silence, reflection, and meditation. Many
saints read a daily regimen of scripture, and then hasten
on with their day. Most Americans are *busy* people, and
thankfully the Spirit is gracious to sometimes steer us *on
the run!* However, it is often in silence or in a devotional
prayerfulness that we become aware of the mind of the
Spirit, urging us, influencing us toward a particular insight,
situation, person, or to a deeper communion with the Lord
Himself. We should value and protect those times.

Someone has said, *'The shepherd doesn't drive his sheep, he
leads them.'* There is great joy in being 'led of the Spirit,' but
it means our inner eyes must be steadily on the One going
before us, attentive and responsive. The great enemies of the
sensitivity we desire are worry, frantic activity, and 21ˢᵗ century *noise.* Even when we become silent we're often overrun

with thoughts of stuff to do, or unnerved by the quietness. We mustn't become discouraged; we're all just children.

Embrace the holy process of "grow(ing) in the grace and knowledge of our Lord and Savior Jesus Christ." (2 Peter 3:18) Enjoying a life under the administration of the Spirit requires time, practice, patience, humility, and faith. But the grace received by expending these produces far more than any frenzied busy-ness. Taking long walks in the woods helped me begin this discovery. Over time, we learn to 'go with what we know;' not acting *irrationally*, but sometimes *supra*-rationally; guided and enlightened by the Holy Spirit. We should depend on those transactions, sometimes daily, hourly.

Living under the leadership of the Holy Spirit doesn't free us from the inevitable conflict between the persistent weakness of our human nature and our desire to please God. Paul details this conflict very candidly in Romans seven, a passage all of us should revisit regularly! We will never outlive the need for repentance. *"If we say we have no sin, we deceive ourselves, and the truth is not in us. If we confess our sins, He is faithful and just to forgive us our sins and to cleanse us from all unrighteousness."* (1 John 1:8, 9)

One of the great challenges we face is endeavoring to help others with their issues, all the while being disturbed by our *own* weaknesses. "The just shall live by his faith" is quite plainly the simple truth. We are not buoyed along by our spotless performance, but rather we are the glad recipients of God's unmerited grace every day, allowing us to joyfully serve in His name in spite of our sometimes contrary selves. In the end our testimony will surely be how God rescued us again and again; a fact that makes worship and praise a most personal and profound delight!

No one will discern the mind of the Spirit perfectly. I've been mistaken plenty of times, but if we determine to err on the side of love and peace, generosity and humility, our sincere efforts will be constructive in some way . . . and we will learn from it. Even Jesus *"increased in wisdom and stature, and in favor with God and men."* We can be secure knowing we have a Teacher who will faithfully instruct and enlighten us all our lifetime. (1 Cor. 2:9-13)

Every earnest believer, in the final analysis, will be the beneficiary of God's great providence, seeing to it that we stumble into the place we need to be, or bump into the contact that will help us get where we're going. I'm so grateful for those times when I was trying my best to sense God's leading without finding clarity, and He literally pushed me through the right door!

A Window into You

You are the Plan reminds us that by His grace the saints have become, *you* have become, the center of His redemptive activity. Of course it is God's purpose to extend redemption to the entire world, and precisely because we all have a part in that, His *immediate* concern is getting you and I thoroughly converted! This does not make any of us spiritual 'big shots;' it is the humbling reality behind the fact that *Jesus died for me!*

3. Finally, I want to emphasize the importance of our desires as a guidepost for our journey. Our desires, or inner motivations, are a strategic part of our makeup, and as such, they are an area where God quite often deposits vision or

intent that is *kingdom specific*. Often this part of our humanity is under-appreciated or subordinated to more practical,
urgent, or 'spiritual' matters; sometimes necessary in the
short-term, but a critical mistake in the larger context of
our life-long journey with the Lord.

God's dealing with you will be similar to His interaction with others in some general ways, but in the particular area of desires and motivations, the things that
move you, His commerce with you may be very unique.
Value that. Since we all experience the Holy Spirit differently, the *desires* you discover within might indeed
be a voice and language of the Spirit you more easily
comprehend.

Many Christian traditions which do not present the Holy
Spirit in personal terms will, at the same time, encourage a
genuine responsiveness to one's desires, or 'inner compass,' as
a legitimate expression of 'the Spirit.' They realize the Lord
wants His people to have a keen awareness of His deposit in
their lives, and to give a willing response to those inner activities which they regard as having a divine origin. One's *desires*
can quite easily fit that description.

Challenging our Freedom

When we begin to speak of our desires, we are com-
pelled to also talk about *freedom*. Without doubt, this
is a difficult and very sensitive area for many of God's
people.

We all witness bondage every day. Not the kind involving ropes, chains, and bars, but those terrible con-
finements of personality and spirit which keep otherwise
healthy human beings from responding meaningfully to

the many opportunities for self-expression and explora-
tion they might enjoy. Many people are not free to act, or
speak, or participate, or dissent, or explore, or change, or
be how and what they want to be. Impeding them are a
host of thoughts, feelings, opinions, taboos, and perceived
limitations which effectively paralyze them. Sadly, many
of these folks so affected are genuine Christians.

So, the need to cultivate and pray for personal freedom
is very great. In most instances, healthy believers should
be free to respond to God, and to the people, needs, situ-
ations, and opportunities surrounding them. They should
enjoy the liberty to think, to obey, to move, to start and to
stop; to wait without anxiety and to go without hesitation
under the Spirit's leadership. It is easy to see how the quo-
tient of freedom every saint holds is significant in being
God's plan.

Freedom is not an entity in itself; it is dependent on
other concrete realities for its existence, much like a shadow
or an eclipse. In our context, the things that give freedom
its definition are **desires** and **destination.** For example,
let us suppose I put a leg-chain on you and fastened it to a
tree. As long as you are content to sit under that tree, your
bonds and the resulting lack of freedom will never be an
issue for you. When you decide to move is precisely when
your freedom, or lack of it, becomes evident.

Many believers are in varying degrees of bondage but
never fully apprehend the fact, perhaps because they have
few desires, or they devalue them, and they have no particular destination. Therefore, freedom is pretty meaning-
less. They may like to talk about freedom, but for them
it is purely a matter of language and symbolism, a word

with comfortable connotations. The Apostle Paul wrote to the Romans (1:13), *"I often planned to come to you, but I was hindered until now."* How did Paul recognize the hindrance? Because he had an identified destination, and his desire to reach it gave definition to the hindrance.

One great way to measure your real freedom is to accept the challenge of one of your desires.

Desires are intrinsic to the Christian life. We may be particularly responsive to those desires which emerge in us shortly after we meet the Lord. Examples might be a desire to learn and teach the Word, or do missions work, to serve the needy, or to write music for worship. Other people might find new motivation to pursue a helping profession, start a business or service organization, learn a new skill or technology, or to visit a certain place or travel the world. But they have this in common: *they are desires directly attributable to our contact with the Kingdom and Spirit of God.* I call these **Defining Desires.** They will always be an important part of our life of faith, and as long as we continue to follow the Lord, most of us will discover they rarely diminish or change very much.

The Bible says a number of significant things about desires. *"Delight yourself in the Lord and He will give you the desires of your heart."* Psalm 37:4 *"Whatever things you desire when you pray, believe..."* Mark 11:24 KJV. However, those *particular* desires birthed by one's experience with God demonstrate His ongoing involvement in the development of the most fundamental parts of our human construct, thereby affecting all of life.

So, it is most important that we identify and act on our defining desires. In other words, they must be regarded as *authoritative*. In fact, they may be important pieces of the map for our journey, and therefore we cannot disregard them any more than we would disregard the Word of God. That is not to say we equate the authority of our desires with the authority of scripture, any more than we would equate the authority of the Sheriff with that of the President. Nonetheless, each plays a role in our lives, and sometimes it's just hard to get in touch with the President.

The key here is finding the capacity or courage to act; to do something based on your desires. It doesn't matter what that desire is, *do something with it!* For example, if you're motivated to feed the hungry, start planning now to fix dinner for a needy family. If you want to take a mission trip, go today to the U.S. Post Office nearest you, and apply for a passport. If you want to see the Grand Canyon, get on-line to the Flagstaff, Arizona Chamber of Commerce for information and start planning a trip. Whatever it is, something significant awaits you as a result of having acted on your desires. Somewhere in that process many folks set in motion a miracle!

Be careful to appreciate even those desires which, compared with those of other believers, may seem insignificant, or non-spiritual. That's why comparisons are so foolish. (2 Cor. 10:12) Remember the amazing verses in Romans 1; *"But God has chosen the foolish things of the world to put to shame the wise, and God has chosen the weak things of the world to put to shame the things that are mighty . . . "* (vss. 27-29) You and I have no idea where our desires will lead us, who they will bring us in contact with, or how they will fit in the complex of human activity God is using to work out His purposes in the earth. If we rationalize that our desires and motivations are of little consequence to God we may have begun to close the door on our destiny. Value your individuality. Don't worship it, but don't demean it either.

Our desires might direct us toward a business enterprise, public service, politics, environmental issues, health care, something artistic, and on and on. In fact, one desire might be the engine that propels you into another, more meaning-ful pursuit. Whatever it turns out to be, if it involves *engaging or impacting people*, either directly or indirectly, then likely there's a kingdom component to that desire. 5 loaves and 2 fish fed the multitude (John 6:1-14), but if the lad hadn't offered what he had to Jesus, that miracle would not have happened as it did. Perhaps we should treat our defining de-sires as our 'loaves and fish' on the journey to destiny. *God is counting on us to present what we have.* Destiny is not in the hands of fate, but in the hands of men and women who can choose.

God has placed us strategically in His Kingdom, but His purposes for us, strangely enough, are hidden among that tan-gle of grocery lists, chance encounters, birthday parties, stuff in the mail, burning the leaves, and praying for an extra hun-dred dollars before Friday. As we patiently pursue our defin-ing desires, sometimes over years, *even decades*, we may expect God to appear at some unexpected place or time, sometimes upending the present agenda, and unveiling something good we could have never anticipated!

Of course there are always family members, friends, and well-meaning saints who will try to dissuade us. They can't see anything in our particular desire or motivation that is 'worthy,' or recognized as an 'approved' pursuit within their group. We should expect challenges of that sort, and be prepared to patiently explore our freedom with grace and perseverance. Issues of money, health, responsibilities, and difficult relationships can also curb our ability to pursue those desires, and in some cases can completely stifle them. When that happens we must bring those desires before the Lord and offer them as we would our worship, trusting Him to receive the frustration or disappointment that accompanies them, and to redirect our hearts toward another constructive and fulfilling end. He's got lots of stuff in His bag.

I have great sympathy for those people in our lives who oppose almost everything; who pray things never change, or never get hairy, who never want to be inconvenienced, or extended, or to feel used. People who pray things never change often die long before they die, and die before their time! By the same token, folks who see life as a journey toward God, with changing landscapes and diverse seasons, who risk, and dream, and plan, and pray, and try hard, live richer and longer. By the grace of God, and as you're able, identify and seize those defining desires, and let them help carry you further into His holy purposes!

***You* are the Plan**. The stuff that makes you a valuable part of the kingdom of God is already in you, by genetics, by your experiences (good and bad), and by the Holy Spirit living in you. There is no mysterious 'plan of God' for your life apart from the multifaceted grace and goodness of God revealed to you as you walk with Him, doing those things life requires of us all; work and worship, food and rest, relationships and recreation.

With the support of the Word and the Spirit, willingly fulfill your responsibilities, try hard to maintain your integrity, and seize your freedom to act on the motivations and desires that are in your mind and heart. Most of those desires will be confirmed, encouraged, or refined by other Spirit-led individuals. As you continue to live and pray under the Spirit's direction you'll be strengthened and fortified, and He will, moment to moment, recalibrate your course, and keep you in Jesus' love and peace. (Jude 20) *That's the plan of God for your life.*

"*Whoever will save his life will lose it, but whoever will lose his life for my sake will find it again.*" There, another example of Jesus saying it better, with less effort.

But it's not about you

Ultimately everyone's life is *about* something. It may be a career, another person, a recreation, a hobby, a crusade, or even a grievance. It's the thing they live for, the thing that gets them up in the morning, their 'reason to be.' **You are the Plan** is actually a simple statement of God's invitation and intent to make your life and mine *all about Jesus Christ.*

Nevertheless, there will undoubtedly be Christians who will choose not to approve or embrace **You are the Plan**. "*That sounds kind of trendy; too much like a fad or a gimmick for me!*" We must be careful not to expect everyone to see and evaluate things as we do. That would be contrary to much of what we're saying here.

To some people **You are the Plan** may sound intimidating, putting them under a perceived pressure to interact more closely with God. Not everyone is comfortable with that. They prefer a Christianity that is a belief system, and out of that system grows a religious practice that affords them fellowship, accountability, absolution from sin, and the assurance of heaven when they die.

They've believed the gospel and confessed Jesus as their Savior, but walking by the Spirit is something they've not been able to grasp, or really *see* for their own lives. God does not *compel* us to relate to Him in a precise way. "My yoke is easy, My burden is light," Jesus promised.

Other Christians, upon hearing **You are the Plan**, may find it intriguing, but it also sounds somewhat exhausting to them; a kind of spiritual triathlon. They simply *prefer* the more leisurely socio-spiritual framework that institutional religion generally provides; the clergy, contacts, activities, pageants, and structured worship experience. They've sought out a venue that is most comfortable or seems the right 'fit' for them. Again, that's a widely accepted way to function in American Christian culture. In other words, for the most part, let someone else be 'the plan.'

Of course, gravitating toward any teaching that affirms great personal freedoms will be damaged, disturbed, or dysfunctional individuals who try to use it as a license for inappropriate behaviors. Paul's great freedom letter to the Galatians warned of this. *"For you, brethren, have been called to liberty, only do not use liberty as an opportunity for the flesh, but through love serve one another."* (5:13)   His antidote was *"Walk in the Spirit, and you will not fulfill the lust (demands) of the flesh."* (5:16)   However, we all know well-intentioned souls who are unable to govern their tendencies to promote themselves or manipulate others. Healthy, Spirit-led believers must be prepared to offer loving guidance and correction to those who misapply these freedoms, and ignore the responsibilities inherent in being God's instrument.

Finally, some believers may view **You are the Plan** as rather narcissistic or humanistic, perhaps self-exalting, or at the least an ill-advised detour from Christian orthodoxy. To them it presents a faith and practice that is far too independent, dangerously loosed

from the moorings of more *legitimate* Christian doctrine and practice. It appears to be taking away from the proper focus on Jesus
Christ, and diverting it toward ourselves.

In that case, let's be clear. Christianity *is* Jesus Christ.
Redemption is the primary theme of the Bible, and Jesus Christ is
the heart of that glorious process, both for the individual and for
the whole world. His life, death, and resurrection, His story is 'the
gospel.'

Paul told the Colossians that *"in all things He should have the pre-
eminence,"* and that *"by Him all things are held together."* He told the
Philippians that *"at the name of Jesus every knee shall bow . . . and that
every tongue should confess that Jesus Christ is Lord."* In no sense are we
to diminish the fact that *"of Him, and to Him, and through Him are all
things."*

Yet it is evident from scripture that the sacrificial death of
Jesus on the cross was no end in itself. It was God's eternal means
to bring about the cleansing and rehabilitation of a creation taken
captive by sin and Satan, and the beginning and centerpiece of
that great redemptive process is the regeneration of human beings.
(Romans 8:18-21) Far from diminishing the glory of Jesus Christ,
men and women who realize the plan of God is for them to live
and walk in His Spirit actually become the vehicles to make His
living presence and glory known. *"He will glorify Me,"* Jesus said of
the Spirit, and the greater liberty and authority we give the Spirit in
our lives the more people will see Jesus in and though us.

Rather than diverting attention *away* from Jesus Christ, **You
are the Plan** focuses our entire existence on His interests. It
doesn't allow us to live on the outskirts of kingdom activity. It
suggests we are at the epicenter of God's doings, bringing gospel
resources to the streets and marketplaces of our world. By our
prayerful presence within society's daily commerce, the eternal

light shines everywhere, on everyone. That's our place, our privilege; that's the plan.

I want to reemphasize what I said in the introduction. **You are the Plan** should not be viewed as adversarial to organized Christianity. Rather, I suggest it is the very thing the churches and ministries are commissioned to promote; *"(God has) raised us up together, and made us sit together in the heavenly places in Christ Jesus, that in the ages to come He might show the exceeding riches of His grace in His kindness toward us in Christ Jesus . . . . for we are His workmanship, created in Christ Jesus for good works, which God prepared beforehand that we should walk in them." (Eph. 2: 6, 7, 10)*

Paul's letters repeatedly affirm the goal of every Christian endeavor; to instruct, equip, and help empower the saints to reflect the spirit and ministry of Jesus as they walk in freedom and fellowship with their Father. As I've said before, when the churches are *actually doing this*, they are a blessing and a most valuable kingdom resource; indeed a *sanctuary* for God's people. Obviously, many saints and leaders feel *called* to serve within the organized church. Again, *"God has set the members, each one of them, in the body just as He pleased."* (1 Cor. 12:18) Our purpose here is not to play God in people's lives, but to encourage them to follow His leading wherever, and with whomever He pleases.

However, we should not make what is 'typical' Christian practice our reference point. Paul urged the Philippians to heed the 'upward call' of the Spirit, and challenged them to walk consistent with the highest revelation and understanding they had attained. (Phil. 3:14-16) If and when **You are the Plan** resonates with your heart and aligns with your grasp of the scriptures, then I urge you to seize on it with vigor and vision. The Spirit will doubtless lead you in precisely where, and with whom, to walk it out, whether in the established churches, with some other community of 'the faith,' or through a unique calling that may be outside the norms and, to some folks, difficult to understand. Remember Paul's defense of liberty; *"Who are you to judge another's servant? To his own master he stands or falls. Indeed, he will be made to stand, for God is able to make him stand."* (Rom. 14:4)

It has not been my aim to explain how redemption (conversion) and spiritual growth happens. There are many great resources which clearly detail that wonderful process in scriptural and practical terms. I have also purposefully avoided discussing the many liberating truths that are realized through a relationship with Jesus Christ. My intent has been select and simple; to persuade men and women they need not 'discover' a plan of God for their lives apart from their daily contact with the Spirit, the Word, and the brethren, and their response to each of them in faith and purpose. Again, that *is* the plan of God. Many writings of the old saints clearly point out that God's real joy is in sharing the journey with us, not in our attaining a particular destination or achievement. In fact, ultimately, *He is the destination!*

Both scripturally and practically, God's redemptive plan for mankind is best carried forward by the saints in the complex of daily life. People touching people, allowing the Word in them to "become flesh" (John 1:14) so that the gospel is not only heard, but is first *seen*, giving weight to the Word spoken or preached. We've seen from the scriptures and from experience that God works mostly through *process*, not titanic events. Godly men and women, families, are the clear witness to His redeeming grace, and to His interaction with us along the time line. We testify of the resurrection by our own transformation and spiritual radiance, and consequently sinners are converted through the inner invitation of the

Father as they associate with us and share our journey. (John 6:44)
Our purpose is to help everyone in our world discover the rich-
ness of spiritual life and fellowship in this kingdom that is "close
at hand." (Matt. 3:17)

13

STEPPING UP

The gospel illustrated through a believer's everyday experience is the clearest, and most digestible form it can take.

In his interesting book on the Protestant reformation, "The Dividing of Christianity," author Christopher Dawson analyzed the movement from the Catholic point of view. Paying tribute to St. Ignatius Loyola, founder of the Jesuits, and leader of the Catholic counter-reformation, he referred to them this way: *"They were unknown men, with no interests to defend, who were uncommitted to the mistakes of the past."* I've seized that description to challenge ordinary men and women to become difference makers in the church's future!

If there is to be any substantive change in the collective understanding and practice of life-in-Christ in the American church, it will necessarily come from 'the ground up,' not the top down. It is difficult to envision our institutions, denominations, and various sects all coming to a place of genuine unity of spirit and purpose.

Any human effort toward that end would involve decades of discussion and debate, which most usually becomes the genesis for
yet another 'movement.'

Many believers and leaders express hope for a sweeping na-
tional 'revival,' even a global one; some kind of divine revelation
that stirs the saints to greater devotion and unity, and sinners to
repent. But what that would actually look like we can only speculate, though we may surely hope and pray for it. I don't think for
a moment God has given up on the world. *"The earth shall be full
of the knowledge of the Lord as the waters cover the sea."* (Isaiah 11:9) I
fervently believe that promise, but just *how* the glorious fulfillment
of it will take place is yet hidden in God's mind.

However, there *is* a call from the Spirit for the saints to simply
begin to live as 'the plan of God.' If there is any positive change *we*
can effect, it is possible primarily on the individual level, as Spirit-
filled men and women embrace the adventure of being pioneers,
paving the way for new expressions of God's church throughout
the world.

Again, we must begin by taking *ownership of the gospel.* That
does not require creating a 'manual' or a set of approved guidelines
for everyone's witness. Even in the New Testament church there
were at least two 'gospels' being preached, one configured for the
Jewish church and another for the gentile churches (Gal. 2:7, 8).
Uniformity of presentation or precise content isn't required, but
simply a uniformity of passion for Jesus Christ. Paul rejoiced the
gospel was being preached even with questionable motives and in
a contentious spirit (Phil. 1:15-18).

Genuinely converted men and women have biblical authority
to speak of the things concerning Jesus Christ in the language and
understanding God has given them. The Holy Spirit can clean up

the details later; our task is to boldly proclaim the message that "is the power of God to salvation for everyone who believes . . ." (Rom. 1:16).

What will this 'Christianity' look like?

Perhaps the best (though oversimplified) answer; *it will look like home*. In other words, a Christianity exemplified and facilitated by ordinary believers will necessarily find its context and character in the real world of families, friends, homes, shops, and neighborhoods. It will not require a uniform, a vernacular, an authority structure, or a special facility. To say the kingdom of God has 'drawn near,' is to simply state, "*He has come to us; He is wherever we are.*" God among His people in the most literal and practical sense.

Jesus words do not suggest the need for a specific place to house kingdom activity. Sharing a meal, working on a project, celebrating a new baby, retrieving the cows that got out; these are all real-life events that bring people together, and the result is the sharing of our lives. Christian people welcome these occasions to bear witness to God's goodness and sustaining grace along the time-line. And often, when all has been said and done, something like *church* will have happened.

Of course, life is not easy or seamless, and neither is the challenge to be 'the plan.' Part of the appeal of institutional religion is that initiative, creativity, and strenuous effort are generally not required for participation. Living the gospel truthfully before neighbors and friends is often challenging, and our very flawed human selves will often be exposed. The risks are multitude, and blunders and disappointments are inevitable. But in the long run that's doubtless healthier for us (and less corrosive) than a

Christianity that bids us take a seat as simply another spectator at Sunday services.

The gospel illustrated through a believer's everyday experience is the clearest, and most digestible form it can take. Observing someone grappling with life's (and *people's*) contrariness in the spirit of Jesus Christ is, to an unbeliever, a window into the kingdom of God. We're not obligated to 'sell' the story, only to tell it, in sincerity and honesty. It won't be perfect or comprehensive, but raw and real. People don't need a detailed explanation of love, or goodness, or faith; when they *see it*, or *experience it*, many of them will recognize in it something rare and valuable and will be eager to close the deal.

To say it another way, this 'Christianity' will *look like you*, and the other saints around you. It will be a 'message in motion,' not confined by doctrine or tradition, but supported by real stuff like godliness, compassion, service, and sacrifice. This Christianity will be neither polished nor pre-packaged, but will have the scars and bruises, the duty-worn tools and the firm grip of blue collar saints, *bringing it* where it's needed most. As a corporate presence, this Christianity is most likely going to resemble a fort on the edge of a wilderness; crude, lean, built from the stuff at hand, but offering welcome sanctuary and supply to pilgrims on their journey. That's how I see it down the road.

There is no 'higher' level of Christian authority to which we may appeal for support or affirmation in this effort. Christian institutions and organizations are merely representations of someone's outlook, agenda, or understanding. They can confer, debate, vote, and pass legislation but they cannot *decide* anything. And there are very few 'elders' whose perspectives are not interfaced with some religious system. Only men and women of the Spirit can decide things, and then act on their decision.

Having said that, I again issue the caution that no Christian should imagine he or she can live a balanced life without the help of others. All of us need the perspectives, wisdom, and example that godly folks provide. *"A man who isolates himself seeks his own desire; he rages against all wise judgment."* (Prov. 18:1) In many cases, much needed guidance and encouragement will come from good and godly souls within the traditional churches. But in the final analysis, the advice and experience we gather from those around us can only take us so far. Ultimately one must decide for himself what the Spirit is asking him to do.

It is much like a young Christian coming to an age when his parents' beliefs and values must either be confirmed in his own experience, or give way to a somewhat different faith and practice formed through his personal engagement with the Word, the church, and the world. Making those choices is usually a challenging and sometimes lengthy process but its resolution is vital to his maturity and future service to the Lord. Nothing of kingdom significance is 'borrowed;' we've got to *own it*!

Going forward, responsible believers must set a positive tone for interaction with all Christians, both inside and outside the institutional churches, and by our attitudes and behaviors earn their love and respect. Paul said we should work hard for "the unity of the Spirit in the bond of peace." (Ephesians 4:3) Exactly *where* one chooses to walk out his faith is a matter of God's leading, one's calling, one's traditions, and the kingdom connections he has established. Mature believers should be comfortable in, and benefit from any truly Christian environment, regardless of how different it might be from their customary practice.

The vision we're setting forth is a radical transformation of the church from the *inside out*, enlisting men and women whose first loyalty is to the interests of Jesus Christ. The Lord's priorities have never been to produce numbers, dollars, and dimensions, but to sustain the grand work of making saints for the increase of His kingdom. That doesn't require real estate, but it does require *real people*. Jesus isn't out to impress anyone, but to satisfy His Father's heart.

But keep in mind, taking ownership of the gospel doesn't in any way imply a step *away* from the organized church, but rather a deliberate step *toward* a more personal and profound engagement with the Holy Spirit and the scriptures. In so doing, one accepts the administration of the Spirit for his life and service, and necessarily, the demands of institutional Christianity are moderated by, and subordinated to the leading of the Spirit. In a perfect world the interests and priorities of the Spirit and the visible church would be synonymous, but that's not always the case. I recall an exceptional example of this from the life of a dear friend now with the Lord.

One Saturday night many years ago Doyle Tucker was summoned to the side of a boyhood friend who had been critically stabbed and was near death. An amazing psalmist, composer, and worship leader, Doyle was scheduled to be at a church of thousands to perform the next morning. Knowing Doyle as we did, there was never much doubt about where he'd be; through the night and into Sunday he was with his friend to the end. Despite his earnest apologies, the church leadership criticized him sharply for upending their program. I've always been proud that my friend didn't elevate his career above his calling and character. Doyle Tucker understood that the Kingdom priority is almost always people, especially *hurting people*. Of course, the church recovered nicely, and I've always hoped they were able to search out what the Spirit had prepared for them that morning in Doyle's absence.

In most cases, however, when we make commitments to *any* community of believers, we should make every effort to fulfill them. Being 'Spirit led' is not a convenient license to be unreliable or irresponsible. None of that nonsense that says, *"Oh I'm sorry! I can't fulfill my pledge because the Spirit just told me to do 'thus and so.'"* In whatever context the servants and saints of God are laboring, they are loved and valued by God, and interaction with them, as much as lies within us, should be with integrity and loving respect.

"By this all will know that you are My disciples, if you have love for one another." (John 13:35) Francis Schaeffer was right when he said the world has no obligation to believe in Jesus Christ *until they can visibly see this*. **You are the Plan** is a foundational understanding that makes this transcendent unity actually possible. When one embraces its intent, he becomes personally responsible to God for his engagement with, and responses to, other believers. He does not first identify them with an organization, creed, or religious class. They, like himself, are the domain of God's Spirit and His holy purposes, so finding a common ground with them leading to unity is paramount to maintaining loyalty to the King.

14

A SAMPLING OF SCRIPTURE

The words of Jesus and the apostles repeatedly affirm the perspective offered by *You are the Plan*. Here are just a few:

> ". . . Work out your own salvation with fear and trembling, for it is God who works in you both to will and to do for His good pleasure." Philippians 2:12, 13

> "You are the salt of the earth . . . You are the light of the world." Matthew 5:13, 14

> "As many as are led by the Spirit of God, these are sons of God." Romans 8:14

> "To them God willed to make known what are the riches of the glory of this mystery among the Gentiles, which is Christ in you, the hope of glory." Colossians 1:27

> "Therefore you shall be perfect, just as your Father in heaven is perfect." Matthew 5:48

"For you died, and your life is hidden with Christ in God. When Christ who is our life appears, then you also will appear with him in glory." Colossians 3:3, 4

"For if by one man's offense death reigned through the one, much more those who receive abundance of grace and of the gift of righteousness will reign in life through the One, Jesus Christ." Romans 5:17

"For all things are yours, whether Paul, or Apollos, or Cephas, or the world or life or death, or things present or things to come – all are yours. And you are Christ's, and Christ is God's." 1 Cor. 3:21-23

"I am the vine, you are the branches. He who abides in Me, and I in him, bears much fruit." Matt. 15:5

"Do not fear, little flock, for it is your Father's good pleasure to give you the kingdom." Luke 12:32

"You are God's field, you are God's building." 1 Corinthians 3:9

"Do you not know you are the temple of God and that the Spirit of God dwells in you?" 1 Corinthians 3:16

"For we are His workmanship, created in Christ Jesus for good works, which God prepared beforehand that we should walk in them." Ephesians 2:10

"He who has begun a good work in you will complete it until the day of Jesus Christ." Philippians 1:6

"For in Him dwells all the fullness of the Godhead bodily, and you are complete in Him, who is the head of all principality and power." Colossians 2:9, 10

"You did not choose Me, but I chose you and appointed you that you should go and bear fruit, and that your fruit should remain, that whatever you ask the Father in My name He may give you." John 15:16

"But you are a chosen generation, a royal priesthood, a holy nation, His own special people, that you may proclaim the praises of Him who called you out of darkness into His marvelous light." 1 Peter 2:9

"Therefore let no one judge you in food or in drink, or regarding a festival or a new moon or Sabbaths, which are a shadow of things to come, but the substance is of Christ." Colossians 2:16, 17

"Now to Him who is able to do exceedingly abundantly above all that we ask or think, according to the power that works in us, to Him be glory in the church by Christ Jesus . . ." Ephesians 3:20

". . . By which have been given to us exceedingly great and precious promises, that through these you may be partakers of the divine nature . . ." 2 Peter 1:4

"Now may the God of peace who brought up our Lord Jesus from the dead . . . make you complete in every good work to do His will, working in you what is well pleasing in His sight, through Jesus Christ, to whom be glory forever and ever." Hebrews 13:20, 21

"Therefore whoever hears these sayings of Mine, and does them, I will liken him to a wise man who built his house on the rock: and the rain descended, the floods came, and the wind blew and beat on that house, and it did not fall, for it was founded on the rock." Matt.7:24, 25

15

A FINAL EXAMPLE

Not since the days of Moses and the crossing of
the Red Sea, when Miriam and the maidens of
Israel sang and danced in celebration, had anyone
seen such a sight.

*"After this I will return and will rebuild the tabernacle of David which has
fallen down. I will rebuild its ruins, and I will set it up, so that the rest of
mankind may seek the Lord, even all the Gentiles (nations) who are called by
My name, says the Lord."* (Amos 9:11, 12)

As the early church leaders began to realize the scope of God's
redemptive work through Jesus Christ, they counselled together
how God's grace should be extended to the non-Jewish believers.
In Acts 15 James, leader of the Jerusalem church, stood among the
brethren and quoted those words from the prophet Amos.

At a most important moment in the formation of the primitive
church, God granted the Apostles wisdom and grace toward the
non-Jewish believers, because their inclusion in Christ was clearly
something of His doing; eternal in its conception and purpose.

(15:18) However, what stirs me deeply is that the prophetic example James used is without doubt the most graphic and potent Old Testament archetype for **You are the Plan.**

More significant than the *symbolic* values in the tabernacle of David is the simple fact that it represents the most passionate and vigorous effort of a single individual to imitate, honor, and celebrate God in all of scripture. (ref: 1 Chron. 15-16, 23:5) Somehow liberated from religious constraints by his gritty and tested relationship with God, worked out on the Judean highlands, David personifies in my mind those famous Sinatra lyrics from 1969, ". . . the record shows I took the blows, and did it my way!"

In the valley of Elah, when he faced Goliath of Gath, David refused the conventional wisdom and weaponry of Israel's best military men, and took down the Philistine with his weapons of choice; a sling, a rock, and a declaration, "The battle is the Lord's!"

When David and his young men were weary and hungry, he persuaded the priest Ahimelech to provide them with the holy 'show bread' from the tabernacle, something forbidden by the law. He was confident his God valued men more than a religious symbol.

Running from the jealous Saul, David fled to the caves at Adullam. Misfits, crazies, and malcontents attached themselves to him in his distress, but his character and leadership shaped those 400 unlikely souls into one of the most brutal fighting forces in recorded history. The exploits of his 'mighty men' sound almost mythological.

Twice he could have killed Saul as he was pursued by him through the rugged terrain of Southern Israel, but against the urging of his men David refused to touch "the Lord's anointed." Integrity far outweighed strategic advantage to 'the man after God's own heart.'

As David and his band pursued the Philistines from Ziklag, after their enemy had ransacked the city, 200 men could not keep pace. David left them by the brook Besor to guard the supplies while He and the others recovered their captured families. On returning to the brook David confounded some of his men by insisting that the spoils of battle be shared equally by all. *"As his part is who goes down to the battle, so shall his part be who stays by the supplies; they shall share alike."* David ignored the ancient military protocols and let his heart assign value to each man's contribution.

More significant, however, than David's reputation as a leader and warrior, was his passion as a worshipper. When he was finally able to bring the Ark of the Covenant to Jerusalem, the opportunity to express his heart for God reached its zenith. For the church in every generation, the restoration of the 'tabernacle of David' is the rediscovery of David's spiritual, cultural, and artistic renaissance among the people of God; a standard and vision for worshippers everywhere!

With holy anticipation, David lined the highway up to Zion with Israel's elders and prominent military and civic leaders, along with Levites and priests, singers, dancers, and musicians. Dressed in priestly attire, the Shepherd-King led the parade as the Ark of the Covenant was escorted home with shouting and horns, trumpets and cymbals, harps and stringed instruments. David danced, and whirled, and played his instrument in an unrestrained celebration before, and unto the Living God. His utter joy at welcoming the Shekinah (Presence) into his city was on display in every conceivable way! Not since the days of Moses and the crossing of the Red Sea, when Miriam and the maidens of Israel sang and danced in celebration, had anyone seen such a sight!

Centuries before *"the veil of the temple was torn in two from top to bottom,"* (Matt. 27:51) David boldly unveiled the Ark of the Covenant and brought it to rest under an open canopy. He had already set about creating an entirely new worship culture to accompany it. He enlisted Asaph, and other gifted psalmists to compose music and lyrics for praising the Lord. He invented new musical instruments for the same purpose, and instituted a regimen of continual celebration on the grounds around the Ark's new dwelling. Stringed instruments and cymbals accompanied songs and shouts of praise to the God of Israel. David's heart overflowed into the very culture of the city and countryside.

It was David's new song that initiated that first great praise service;

> *"Give to the Lord the glory due His name; Bring an offering, and come before Him. Oh, worship the Lord in the beauty of holiness."*
> *"Let the heavens rejoice, and let the earth be glad. And let them say among the nations, 'the Lord reigns.' Oh give thanks to the Lord, for He is good! For His mercy endures forever."*

As you may recall, Israel already enjoyed a highly structured, yet divinely conceived worship form introduced by Moses a thousand years before. As priests and Levites carried out their ceremonial responsibilities on behalf of the people, their sacrifices were accepted, their transgressions were covered, and God's glory was manifested in the Holy of Holies. From the primitive Mosaic perspective, nothing was lacking. But David saw something else.

With David, God looked on a man who delighted in celebrating their relationship *outside* the forms of tabernacle, and Levites, and animal sacrifices. A thousand years before Pentecost David glimpsed the power and provisions of the New Covenant, and lived much of his life responding, not to a religious prescription (holy as it was), but to the movements of God's Spirit upon him and within him. He was clearly the prophet of the apostolic church, quoted more in the early chapters of Acts than any other Old Testament voice.

The responses of David's heart toward God were the hallmark of his forty year reign as king of Israel. Although Solomon's kingdom surpassed David's in scope and grandeur, with opulent Palaces, a magnificent Temple, and indescribable wealth, in God's eyes it never got any better than David's little tent on Zion's hill, with His man, and His people celebrating Him with all their hearts. But that would have never happened if David hadn't somehow awakened to the heart of God, and for one remarkable generation, *actually lived* the Lord's timeless declaration of purpose and freedom over *all* His beloved; ***"You are the Plan!"***